SHIN NIHONGO NO KISO I

ENGLISH TRANSLATION

しんにほんごのきそ I

SHIN NIHONGO NO KISO I

AOTS

ENGLISH TRANSLATION
しんにほんごのきそ I

SHIN NIHONGO NO KISO I

ENGLISH TRANSLATION
しんにほんごのきそⅠ

THE ASSOCIATION FOR OVERSEAS TECHNICAL SCHOLARSHIP (AOTS)

3A Corporation

Shoei Bldg. 6F, 6-3, Sarugaku-cho 2-chome, Chiyoda-ku, Tokyo, 101 Japan

© 3A Corporation 1990

First published in Japan by 3A Corporation 1990

ISBN4-906224-52-0 C0081
Printed in Japan

PREFACE

Since its foundation in 1959, the Association for Overseas Technical Scholarship [AOTS] has devoted itself to accepting and training technical trainees from the developing countries of Asia, Africa and Latin America. By the end of March 1989, the total number of trainees accepted had reached about 40,000, and these trainees had come from over 150 countries around the world.

The biggest problem for trainees staying in Japan and undertaking training in Japanese companies is language. Without a good grasp of Japanese, they cannot get to know and understand Japan, nor can they hope for the best results from their in-company training programmes. We have observed a definite correlation between the results of the training and the trainees' Japanese language ability. We therefore believe AOTS to have been right in stressing the importance of language training for trainees staying in Japan even for a relatively short period.

AOTS's Japanese education programme forms part of the General Orientation Course, which trainees take before undergoing technical training at their sponsor companies. Presently, two General Orientation Courses feature the study of Japanese as one of their major subjects: the six-week course, which has 100 hours of Japanese lessons, and the thirteen-week course, which has 200 hours. The majority of trainees take the six-week course and actually study Japanese for a little under 100 hours. This is an extraordinary short length of time for studying a foreign language. However, considering the trainees' rather limited period of stay and their basic purpose of visiting Japan, as much time as possible must be allocated to the technical training itself. Accordingly, we have done our best to develop the most efficient instruction methods possible; ones that guarantee tangible results in a short period. The outcome is the Japanese instruction methods that we practise at AOTS.

In 1961, we published '*Practical Japanese Conversation*' the first textbook by AOTS. This was followed by a first revised edition in 1964 and a second in 1965. However, in spite of these two revisions, this first generation of textbooks did not fully satisfy AOTS's requirement for Japanese which was 'easy to remember' and 'immediately pratical' while at the same time 'appropriate for technical trainees'.

Then, in 1967, we rewrote and republished '*Practical Japanese Conversation*' from a totally new approach; and, two years later, we completed translating it into five different languages. However, its use in the classroom revealed that it was too comprehensive as a textbook for a 100-hour intensive language course. Further study and analysis then resulted in *NIHONGO NO KISO* (later retitled *NIHONGO NO KISO I*). After this, we introduced *NIHONGO NO KISO II* in 1981 to cater for the increasing number of trainees who had studied Japanese previously and for those on the by-now regularly-held thirteen-week orientation course.

NIHONGO NO KISO I gave many years of good use, and it was assumed that it would continued to be used for some time. However, over ten years have passed since it was first published, and we have seen further diversification of trainees' nationalities and experience of Japanese study over this decade. Thus, in answer to these new requirements, also with the aim of comprehensively reviewing and harmonizing volumes I and II, we started the project of revising the textbooks in 1985. The result of this project, after thorough study and testing, is *SHIN NIHONGO NO KISO I.*

Although, this textbook was specifically compiled for use in AOTS technical trainees, 100-hour Japanese Course, we believe that its clear explanations and instructions will make it extremely useful and practical for all those interested in studying Japanese at the elementary level.

We would like to thank all those who advised us in the preparation of this revision, and we hope that they will continue to support us in making the best possible use of it and in further enhancing AOTS's Japanese education programmes.

November 1989

YAMAMOTO Nagaaki
Director General
The Association for Overseas Technical Scholarship

NOTES ON THE REVISED EDITION

A period of nearly ten years elapsed between the publication of *NIHONGO NO KISO I* and *NIHONGO NO KISO II*, and this led to some inconsistency in the contents. Work on the present revised edition was started in 1985, with the aim of harmonizing the contents of *NIHONGO NO KISO I* and *II* and reflecting our review of our teaching methods. In carrying out the revision, we took the following steps:

1. First, we revised the text contents by re-examining the basic, most frequently-used Japanese sentence patterns, vocabulary and expressions. We also restructured the entire textbook including sentence patterns, example sentences, conversations and exercises.

2. We added a new set of exercises, 'Renshū C', designed to improve learners' practical conversation ability, while retaining the strong points of *NIHONGO NO KISO*, such as better comprehension of sentence patterns and vocabulary through repetition of sentence pattern drills.

3. We investigated the linguistic life of technical trainees, from their arrival in Japan to their departure, with the kind cooperation of the trainees' sponsor companies and training factories. We used the result of this survey to identify the most common situations in which trainees need to speak in Japanese, and reflected these in the textbook's 'Conversation' patterns. These 'Conversations' have been carefully written to provide examples of concise but highly practical and natural Japanese.

4. We tried to make the textbook easy to use for both learners and instructors, with the addition of a review page for each lesson, a grammar summary and a list of related vocabulary.

5. We emphasized the nurturing of listening comprehension at an early stage, with 'drills' providing ample listening practice. Short stories are also provided as an aid to better reading comprehension.

SHIN NIHONGO NO KISO I is therefore an excellent elementary Japanese textbook prepared with the above considerations in mind. It is designed for a total of one hundred hours' study, and has been completed after extensive correction and revision during two years of actual use in the classroom.

In spite of this, however, the Editors are afraid there may still be some deficiencies. Your criticisms and comments will be most welcome and will help us to continue to improve subsequent editions.

EXPLANATORY NOTES

Ⅰ. Structure

The learning materials consist of a Main Text, a supplementary Text and a set of cassette tapes. The Main Text is available in Romanized and Kanji-Kana Versions. The Supplementary Text is currently available in the following languages: English, Indonesian, Thai, Spanish, Korean and Chinese. Versions in other languages will be published shortly.

The materials have been prepared with the main emphasis on listening and speaking Japanese; they do not provide instruction in reading and writing hiragana, katakana or kanji (chinese characters).

Ⅱ. Content and Method of Use

1. Main Text

1) Japanese pronunciation

This section gives examples of the main points to which attention should be paid. Students should concentrate on the major differences between Japanese and their mother tongue.

2) Classroom expressions, greetings, numerals

Students should practise these throughly, since they are useful for understanding classroom instructions and daily greetings. They appear frequently in the lessons.

3) Lessons

There are 25 lessons, with the following contents:

① Sentence Patterns

Basic sentence patterns given in the order they appear in the rest of the lesson.

② Example Sentences

The basic sentence patterns are expressed as a question and answer dialogue. The use of the sentence patterns is indicated in brief, conversational form, and as many as possible of the adverbs and conjunctions dealt with in the lesson are presented. The dialogue includes other learning points besides the basic sentence patterns.

③ Conversation

Typical conversations among trainees staying at an AOTS Training Centre on a six-week orientation course, from the start of the course to their departure for sponsor companies for technical training. The conversations include everyday expressions such as greetings. They are written in plain conversational style and should be learnt by heart. If time allows, students should develop their conversational ability with the Vocabulary Chart and audio-visual aids.

④ Drills

The drills are divided into three levels, A, B and C. Level-A drills are arranged for easy understanding of the grammatical structure and are laid out so as to aid visual memory. They help the student to establish an understanding of the basic sentence patterns through word substitution, and give practice in the use of different forms and conjunctions.

Level-B drills use various drill patterns to strengthen students' grasp of the basic sentence forms. Numbers with a ☞ sign indicate drills which use a Pictorial Chart. Level-C drills are short conversation-style drills, intended for use after students have mastered the basic sentence patterns, through Drills A and B. They are designed to show how the sentence patterns function in actual situations, as well as enhancing students' oral ability.

These drills should not simply be read aloud as written, or merely repeated. It is desirable to practise in a variety of ways by making substitutions suitable to the students' level.

⑤ **Practice Problems**

Two kinds of problems are given; one type for listening practice (🔲) and another for grammar practice. The listening practice problems on the cassette tape are further divided into question and answer problems and questions about the key points of conversations. The listening practice problems are designed to strengthen students' aural ability, while the grammar problems check comprehension of vocabulary and the grammar points from the lessons studied. The reading comprehension problems mostly require the student to give a true/false response after reading a simple sentence compiled from previously-studied words and sentence patterns.

⑥ **Review**

This is provided to enable students to go over the essential points from each lesson.

⑦ **Summary**

At the end of the Main Text, a summary is given covering grammatical points such as the use of the particles, verb forms, adverbs and conjunctions appearing in the lessons. Some example sentences are also given.

⑧ **Index**

This includes classroom expressions, greetings, numerals, and the new vocabulary and expressions introduced in each lesson of the Main Text.

2. **Supplementary Text**

The supplementary Text is divided into four **PARTS** I to VI.

① **PART I : Essential Vocabulary**

This lists the words newly introduced in each lesson with their translations. They are also sold in the form of picture cards as teaching aids.

② **PART Ⅱ : Related Vocabulary**

In 13 sections, this part contains useful but not absolutely essential vocabulary.

③ **PART Ⅲ : Translation**

This is an English translation of the following parts in the Main Text:

Pronunciation guide, Classroom expressions, Greetings,

Sentence patterns, Example sentences, Conversation and Summary

④ **PART Ⅳ : Appendices**

The tables contain some additional study material: e. g. numbers, expressions of time, expressions of period, counters, etc.

3. Note on Romanization

1) In general, the Hepburn system of romanization has been used. The syllabic nasal sound is represented by 'n' throughout.

2) Long vowels are indicated as follows:

ā, ii, ū, ei (ē), ō

e.g. **tokei, onēsan**

3) For readability, the text has been transliterated with spaces between words.

Particles are witten separately except when accepted as forming a single unit with the parent word,

e.g. **nanika, desukara**

4) Prefixes, suffixes and counters are usually separated from their parent words by hyphens, and long compound words are broken up by hyphens,

e.g. **o-shigoto, Tanaka-san, 25-sai, hana-ya, benkyō-shimasu**

However, the hyphen is omitted when the compound is regarded as a single unit,

e.g. **hitotsu, hitori, ocha, asagohan, oyasuminasai**

5) Capitals are used at the beginning of sentences and for the initial letters of proper nouns.

6) Foreign names are spelt according to common practice in their country of origin.

7) Some foreign loan words are romanized to approximate their original pronunciation,

e.g. **pātii, fōku**

4. Miscellaneous

Words which can be omitted from a sentence are enclosed in square brackets [ ].

e.g. **Hai, [watashi wa] Rao desu.**

Synonyms are enclosed in round brackets ( ).

e.g. **otearai (toire)**

An alternative word is enclosed in square brockets in boldface 【 】.

e.g. **【Kōhii】 wa ikaga desu ka.**

TO USERS OF THIS TEXTBOOK

1. **Learn each word carefully and practise the sentence patterns by repeating them.**

    The supplementary Text introduces the new words for each lesson. First learn these words well, then work out the correct meaning of the sentence patterns, and then repeat the sentences until you have mastered the pattern. Please speak the sentences aloud, especially when practising "Drills A and B".

2. **Practise the conversation drills thoroughly.**

    Sentence-pattern practice is followed by conversation practice. The "Conversations" have been carefully written to illustrate actual situations in our daily life. Start by practising "Drill C" to get accustomed to the patterns; then study the "Conversations" to pick up words and phrases useful when you encounter such situations in real life.

3. **Listen to the cassette tape repeatedly.**

    To practise both sentence patterns and conversation, and to acquire correct pronunciation and delivery, we suggest that you speak aloud while listening to the tape.

    The tapes are an extremely effective way of enabling you to get used to the sound and speed of Japanese and building up your listening ability.

    This is why we recommend that you listen to the tapes repeatedly.

4. **Always review what you have learnt.**

    So as not to forget what you have learnt in class, always review it the same day. Finally, try the "Problems" to check what you have learnt and test your listening comprehension.

5. **Use what your have learnt.**

    Don't limit your learning to the classroom. Try talking to your friends and acquaintances (Japanese and non-Japanese) using what you have just learnt. Succeeding in making yourself understood will give you an incentive to study more.

    If you follow the above suggestions and complete this textbook, you will have acquired the basic vocabulary and expressions necessary for daily life. Be patient and work hard!

TERMS USED FOR INSTRUCTION

bunpō	ぶんぽう	grammar
hatsuon	はつおん	pronunciation
bun	ぶん	sentence
tango	たんご	word
onsetsu	おんせつ	syllable
boin	ぼいん	vowel
shi'in	しいん	consonant
dai〜ka	だい〜か	lesson 〜
bunkei	ぶんけい	sentence pattern
kaiwa	かいわ	conversation
reibun	れいぶん	example sentence
renshū	れんしゅう	practice
mondai	もんだい	exercise
fukushū	ふくしゅう	review
reigai	れいがい	exception
hantai	はんたい	opposite
hon'yaku	ほんやく	translation
meishi	めいし	noun
dōshi	どうし	verb
i-keiyōshi	いけいようし	i-adjective
na-keiyōshi	なけいようし	na-adjective
joshi	じょし	particle
fukushi	ふくし	adverb
setsuzokushi	せつぞくし	conjunction
sūji	すうじ	numerals
josūshi	じょすうし	counters
gimonshi	ぎもんし	interrogative
kōzokuku	こうぞくく	a set of particular forms (words or phrases) always used after some conjugated forms of verbs or adjectives
genzai	げんざい	present or non-perfect
kako	かこ	past or perfect
kōtei	こうてい	affirmative
hitei	ひてい	negative
-gurūpu	-グループ	-group
-kei (fōmu)	-けい（フォーム）	-form
teinei-tai	ていねいたい	polite style of speech
futsū-tai	ふつうたい	plain style of speech
sakuin	さくいん	index

CONTENTS

PART I

Essential vocabulary

Lesson 1

watashi	わたし	I
watashi-tachi	わたしたち	we
anata	あなた	you
ano hito	あの　ひと	that person, he, she
minasan	みなさん	ladies and gentlemen, all of you
sensei	せんせい	teacher, instructor
kenshūsei	けんしゅうせい	trainee
～san	～さん	Mr. Mrs. Miss
dare (donata)	だれ（どなた）	who ("donata" is the polite of "dare")
hai	はい	yes
iie	いいえ	no
denki	でんき	electricity, electric light
kikai	きかい	machinery
jidōsha	じどうしゃ	automobile, car
konpyūtā	コンピューター	computer
senmon	せんもん	speciality, specialization of study
-sai	―さい	-years old
nan-sai (o-ikutsu)	なんさい（おいくつ）	how old ("o-ikutsu" is the polite of "nan-sai")

Nihon	にほん	Japan
Indo	インド	India
Indoneshia	インドネシア	Indonesia
Kankoku	かんこく	Korea
Chūgoku	ちゅうごく	China
Firipin	フィリピン	Philippines
Tai	タイ	Thailand
Marēshia	マレーシア	Malaysia
~jin	~じん	suffix meaning 'a national' of; e. g. Indo-jin, an Indian

*　　*　　*　　*　　*

Ohayō gozaimasu.
おはよう　ございます。

Good morning.

Hajimemashite.
はじめまして。

How do you do ?
(literal meaning: I am meeting you for the first time. Usually used as the first phrase when introducing oneself.)

Dōzo yoroshiku.
どうぞ　よろしく。

Nice to meet you.
(literal meaning: Please be good to me. Usually used at the end of a self-introduction.)

Lesson 2

kore	これ	this (thing here)
sore	それ	that (thing near you)
are	あれ	that (thing over there)
kono 〜	この〜	this 〜 (here)
sono 〜	その〜	that 〜 (near you)
ano 〜	あの〜	that 〜 (over there)
hon	ほん	book
zasshi	ざっし	magazine
jisho	じしょ	dictionary
nōto	ノート	notebook
kami	かみ	paper
shinbun	しんぶん	newspaper
tegami	てがみ	letter
enpitsu	えんぴつ	pencil
bōrupen	ボールペン	ballpoint pen
shāpu-penshiru	シャープペンシル	propelling pencil
tabako	たばこ	tobacco, cigarette
matchi	マッチ	match
raitā	ライター	(cigarette) lighter
haizara	はいざら	ashtray
kagi	かぎ	key
tokei	とけい	watch, clock
kaban	かばん	bag, briefcase
hako	はこ	box
tēpu-rekōdā	テープレコーダー	tape recorder
denwa	でんわ	telephone

isu	いす	chair
tsukue	つくえ	desk
mado	まど	window
doa	ドア	door
rajio	ラジオ	radio
terebi	テレビ	television
kamera	カメラ	camera
nan	なん	what
sō	そう	so

*   *   *   *   *

Onegai-shimasu.
おねがいします。

Please.
(When asking for a favour)

Dōzo.
どうぞ。

Please. , Here you are.
(When offering someone something)

[Dōmo] arigatō gozaimasu.
[どうも] ありがとう ございます。

Thank you [very much].

A
あ

Oh!, Ah!
(an exclamation used when suddenly remembering or noticing something)

Chotto
ちょっと

a little, for a moment

Matte kudasai.
まって ください。

Please wait.

Chigaimasu.
ちがいます。

No, it isn't. , You are wrong.

5

Lesson 3

koko	ここ	here, this place
soko	そこ	there, that place near you
asoko	あそこ	that place over there
doko	どこ	where
kochira	こちら	this way, polite of "koko"
sochira	そちら	that way, polite of "soko"
achira	あちら	that way, polite of "asoko"
dochira	どちら	which way, polite of "doko"
kyōshitsu	きょうしつ	classroom
shokudō	しょくどう	dining hall, canteen
otearai (toire)	おてあらい（トイレ）	toilet
robii	ロビー	lobby
uketsuke	うけつけ	reception desk
jimusho	じむしょ	office
heya	へや	room
niwa	にわ	garden
[Kenshū] Sentā	[けんしゅう] センター	the centre [for trainees]
erebētā	エレベーター	lift, elevator
uchi	うち	house
kaisha	かいしゃ	company
kuni	くに	country
uriba	うりば	counter, department (in a department store)

-kai	ーかい	-th floor
-en	ーえん	-yen
ikura	いくら	how much
hyaku	ひゃく	a hundred
sen	せん	a thousand
-man	ーまん	ten thousand
Amerika	アメリカ	the United States
Igirisu	イギリス	Britain, the United Kingdom

* * * * *

[Chotto] sumimasen.
 [ちょっと] すみません。

Excuse me.

Dōmo.
 どうも。

Thank you.
(literal meaning: very much. Used alone, it expresses casual thanks.)

Irasshai[mase].
 いらっしゃい[ませ]。

Welcome. May I help you?
(a greeting to a customer or a guest entering a shop, restaurant, hotel, etc.)

Ja
 じゃ

Well. O.K.

【Kore】o kudasai.
 【これ】を ください。

Please give me【this】.

Lesson 4

okimasu	おきます	get up
nemasu	ねます	sleep, go to bed
hatarakimasu	はたらきます	work
yasumimasu	やすみます	take a rest, take a holiday
benkyō-shimasu	べんきょうします	study
owarimasu	おわります	finish
ima	いま	now
-ji	ーじ	-o'clock
-fun (-pun)	ーふん（ーぷん）	-minutes
han	はん	half past
nan-ji	なんじ	what time
nan-pun	なんぷん	how many minutes
gozen	ごぜん	a.m. , morning
gogo	ごご	p.m. , afternoon
asa	あさ	morning
hiru	ひる	day time, noon
ban (yoru)	ばん（よる）	night, evening
ototoi	おととい	the day before yesterday
kinō	きのう	yesterday
kyō	きょう	today
ashita	あした	tomorrow
asatte	あさって	the day after tomorrow
kesa	けさ	this morning
konban	こんばん	tonight

maiasa	まいあさ	every morning
maiban	まいばん	every night
mainichi	まいにち	every day
Nihon-go	にほんご	the Japanese language
benkyō	べんきょう	study (noun)
kōgi	こうぎ	lecture
kengaku	けんがく	(factory) visit for study and observation
～kara	～から	from～
～made	～まで	up to ～, until～
nichi-yōbi	にちようび	Sunday
getsu-yōbi	げつようび	Monday
ka-yōbi	かようび	Tuesday
sui-yōbi	すいようび	Wednesday
moku-yōbi	もくようび	Thursday
kin-yōbi	きんようび	Friday
do-yōbi	どようび	Saturday
nan-yōbi	なんようび	What day of the week

*　　*　　*　　*　　*

Sō desu ka. そうですか。	I see. (When making agreeable responses)
Taihen desu ne. たいへんですね。	It must be hard for you. (When expressing appreciation or sympathy)

Lesson 5

ikimasu	いきます	go
kimasu	きます	come
kaerimasu	かえります	go home, return
kōjō	こうじょう	factory
eki	えき	railway station
ginkō	ぎんこう	bank
byōin	びょういん	hospital
depāto	デパート	department store
sūpā	スーパー	supermarket
hon-ya	ほんや	bookshop
～ya	～や	～store
-gatsu	ーがつ	-th month of the year
nan-gatsu	なんがつ	what month
tsuitachi	ついたち	first day of the month
futsuka	ふつか	second, two days
mikka	みっか	third, three days
yokka	よっか	fourth, four days
itsuka	いつか	fifth, five days
muika	むいか	sixth, six days
nanoka	なのか	seventh, seven days
yōka	ようか	eighth, eight days
kokonoka	ここのか	ninth, nine days
tōka	とおか	tenth, ten days
jū yokka	じゅうよっか	fourteenth, fourteen days
hatsuka	はつか	twentieth, twenty days
ni-jū yokka	にじゅうよっか	twenty fourth, twenty-four days
-nichi	ーにち	-th day of the month, -days

nan-nichi	なんにち	which day of the month how many days	
itsu	いつ	when	
senshū	せんしゅう	last week	
konshū	こんしゅう	this week	
raishū	らいしゅう	next week	
sengetsu	せんげつ	last month	
kongetsu	こんげつ	this month	
raigetsu	らいげつ	next month	
kyonen	きょねん	last year	
kotoshi	ことし	this year	
rainen	らいねん	next year	
tanjōbi	たんじょうび	birthday	
hikōki	ひこうき	aircraft	
fune	ふね	ship	
densha	でんしゃ	electric train	
basu	バス	bus	
takushii	タクシー	taxi	
chikatetsu	ちかてつ	subway	
shinkansen	しんかんせん	the Shinkansen, the bullet train	
aruite	あるいて	on foot	
hito	ひと	person	
tomodachi	ともだち	friend	
koibito	こいびと	sweetheart	
hitori de	ひとりで	alone	
-bansen	ーばんせん	platform - , -th platform.	

Lesson 6

tabemasu	たべます	eat
nomimasu	のみます	drink
suimasu	すいます	smoke [a cigarette]
[tabako o〜]	[たばこを〜]	
kakimasu	かきます	write, draw, paint
yomimasu	よみます	read
kikimasu	ききます	listen
mimasu	みます	see, look at, watch
kaimasu	かいます	buy
torimasu	とります	take [a photograph]
[shashin o〜]	[しゃしんを〜]	
jisshū-shimasu	じっしゅうします	do practical training
shimasu	します	play [table tennis]
[pinpon o〜]	[ピンポンを〜]	
shimasu	します	do
aimasu	あいます	meet [a friend]
[tomodachi ni〜]	[ともだちに〜]	
gohan	ごはん	a meal, cooked rice
asagohan	あさごはん	breakfast
hirugohan	ひるごはん	lunch
bangohan	ばんごはん	supper
pan	パン	bread
tamago	たまご	egg
niku	にく	meat
sakana	さかな	fish
yasai	やさい	vegetable
ringo	りんご	apple
gyūnyū (miruku)	ぎゅうにゅう（ミルク）	milk
ocha	おちゃ	green tea
kōhii	コーヒー	coffee
kōcha	こうちゃ	black tea
jūsu	ジュース	juice

biiru	ビール	beer
[o-]sake	[お]さけ	alcohol, Japanese rice wine
mizu	みず	water
nekutai	ネクタイ	necktie
shatsu	シャツ	shirt
kutsu	くつ	shoes
tēpu (kasetto-tēpu)	テープ(カセット テープ)	(cassette) tape
firumu	フィルム	film
shashin	しゃしん	photograph
eiga	えいが	movie
pinpon	ピンポン	ping-pong, table tennis
nani	なに	what
issho ni	いっしょに	together
sorekara	それから	after that, and then
~to~	~と~	and
		(conjunction used with nouns)

13

*   *   *   *   *

Moshi moshi	Hello.
もしもし	(on the telephone)
Ā	Ah.
ああ	
【Ashita】 hima desu ka.	Are you free 【tomorrow】?
【あした】 ひまですか。	
Ē	Yes
ええ	
Ii desu ne.	That's good.
いいですね。	
Wakarimashita.	I see. , O.K.
わかりました。	
Mata ashita.	See you tomorrow.
また あした。	

Lesson 7

kirimasu	きります	cut
shūri-shimasu	しゅうりします	repair
kakemasu	かけます	make a phone call
[denwa o~]	[でんわを~]	
agemasu	あげます	give
moraimasu	もらいます	receive
oshiemasu	おしえます	teach
naraimasu	ならいます	learn
kashimasu	かします	lend
karimasu	かります	borrow
hashi	はし	chopsticks
naifu	ナイフ	knife
fōku	フォーク	fork
supūn	スプーン	spoon
hasami	はさみ	scissors
doraibā	ドライバー	screwdriver
supana	スパナ	spanner, wrench
penchi	ペンチ	cutting pliers
okane	おかね	money
purezento	プレゼント	present, gift
repōto	レポート	report

kazoku	かぞく	family
otōsan	おとうさん	father
okāsan	おかあさん	mother
oniisan	おにいさん	elder brother
onēsan	おねえさん	elder sister
otōto	おとうと	younger brother
imōto	いもうと	younger sister
okusan	おくさん	(someone else's) wife
kanai	かない	(one's own) wife
shujin	しゅじん	(one's own) husband
go-shujin	ごしゅじん	(someone else's) husband
kodomo	こども	child
Eigo	えいご	the English language
～go	～ご	～language
mō	もう	already
mada	まだ	not yet
korekara	これから	Soon, from now on

*   *   *   *   *

Omedetō gozaimasu.
おめでとう　ございます

Congratulations.
(for birthday, marriage, New
Year's Day, etc.)

Wā
わあ

wow, oh
(expression of surprise)

Dō itashimashite.
どう　いたしまして。

Never mind. , Not at all.
You are welcome.

Ii【shatsu】desu ne.
いい　【シャツ】ですね。

It's a nice【shirt】,isn't it ?

Lesson 8

kirei [na]	きれい [な]	beautiful, clean
hansamu [na]	ハンサム [な]	handsome
shinsetsu [na]	しんせつ [な]	kind
yūmei [na]	ゆうめい [な]	famous
genki [na]	げんき [な]	healthy, sound, cheerful
shizuka [na]	しずか [な]	quiet
nigiyaka [na]	にぎやか [な]	lively
ōkii	おおきい	big, large
chiisai	ちいさい	small, little
atarashii	あたらしい	new
furui	ふるい	old (not of age)
ii (yoi)	いい (よい)	good
warui	わるい	bad
atsui	あつい	hot
samui	さむい	cold, chilly (weather)
tsumetai	つめたい	cold (temperature)
muzukashii	むずかしい	difficult
yasashii	やさしい	easy
takai	たかい	expensive, tall, high
yasui	やすい	cheap
hikui	ひくい	low
omoshiroi	おもしろい	interesting
oishii	おいしい	tasty, delicious
shiroi	しろい	white
kuroi	くろい	black
akai	あかい	red
aoi	あおい	blue
shiken	しけん	examination
shukudai	しゅくだい	homework
tabemono	たべもの	food
sakura	さくら	cherry blossom
hana	はな	flower

16

machi	まち	town, city
yama	やま	mountain
Fujisan	ふじさん	Mt. Fuji
tokoro	ところ	place
dō	どう	how
donna~	どんな~	what kind of~
dore	どれ	which one
taihen	たいへん	very
amari	あまり	not so~ (used in the negative sentence)
soshite	そして	and (connecting sentences)
~ga, ~	~が、~	~, but~

*　　*　　*　　*　　*

Yā
 やあ

Hi!
 (used by males, this is a casual greeting when meeting a friend.)

Shibaraku desu ne.
 しばらくですね。

Long time no see.

O-genki desu ka.
 おげんきですか。

How are you?

Dōzo kochira e.
 どうぞ　こちらへ。

This way, please.

【Kōhii】 wa ikaga desu ka.
 【コーヒー】は　いかがですか。

Won't you have 【a cup of coffee】?
 (used when offering something to drink, etc.)

Itadakimasu.
 いただきます。

Thank you. I accept.
 (said before starting to eat or drink)

Gochisōsama [deshita].
 ごちそうさま[でした]。

That was delicious.
 (Said after finishing a meal.)

Sō desu ne.
 そうですね。

Well let me see.
 (pausing)

17

Lesson 9

wakarimasu	わかります	understand
arimasu	あります	have
suki [na]	すき [な]	like
kirai [na]	きらい [な]	dislike
jōzu [na]	じょうず [な]	good at
heta [na]	へた [な]	poor at
hiragana	ひらがな	Hiragana script
katakana	かたかな	Katakana script
rōmaji	ローマじ	The Roman alphabet
kanji	かんじ	Chinese characters
ryōri	りょうり	dish (cooked food), cooking
kudamono	くだもの	fruit
nomimono	のみもの	drinks
butaniku	ぶたにく *meat*	pork
toriniku	とりにく	chicken
gyūniku	ぎゅうにく	beef
mikan	みかん	orange
banana	バナナ	banana
ongaku	おんがく	music
uta	うた	song
dansu	ダンス	dance
gitā	ギター	guitar
supōtsu	スポーツ	sport
sakkā	サッカー	soccer
tenisu	テニス	tennis
jikan	じかん	time

takusan	たくさん	many, much
sukoshi	すこし	a little, a few
yoku	よく	well
daitai	だいたい	almost, roughly
zenzen	ぜんぜん	not at all (used in a negative sentence)
mochiron	もちろん	of course
dōshite	どうして	why
~kara	～から	because ~
byōki	びょうき	illness
kusuri	くすり	medicine
atama	あたま	head
onaka	おなか	stomach
itai [atama ga~]	いたい [あたまが~]	have a [head]ache
netsu ga arimasu	ねつが あります	have a fever
kaze o hikimashita	かぜを ひきました	have caught a cold
yasumimasu [kaisha o~]	やすみます [かいしゃを~]	take a day off [from the company]

19

*   *   *   *   *

Nan desu ka.
なんですか。

May I help you ?

Sumimasen ga,
すみませんが、

Excuse me, but~

Dō shimashita ka.
どう しましたか。

What's the matter (with you)?

Lesson 10

imasu	います	exist, be (referring to living things)
arimasu	あります	exist, be (referring to inanimate things)
iroiro[na]	いろいろ[な]	various
ue	うえ	on, above
shita	した	under, below, beneath
mae	まえ	front
ushiro	うしろ	back, behind
migi	みぎ	right (side)
hidari	ひだり	left (side)
naka	なか	in, inside
soto	そと	outside
tonari	となり	next (door)
aida	あいだ	between, among
chikaku	ちかく	near
mono	もの	thing
chizu	ちず	map
keshigomu	けしゴム	eraser
serotēpu	セロテープ	sellotape, clear adhesive tape
hotchikisu	ホッチキス	stapler
pasupōto	パスポート	passport
beddo	ベッド	bed
otoko no hito	おとこの　ひと	man
onna no hito	おんなの　ひと	woman
otoko no ko	おとこの　こ	boy
onna no ko	おんなの　こ	girl

resutoran	レストラン	restaurant
kōen	こうえん	park
taishikan	たいしかん	embassy
yūbinkyoku	ゆうびんきょく	post office
posuto	ポスト	post box
biru	ビル	building
gakkō	がっこう	school
～ya～	～や～	～and ～and so on

* * * * *

Anō
あのう

Excuse me, but...
(used when talking to someone with hesitation)

Itte mairimasu.
いって　まいります。

I'm going to leave now.
(an expression used by a person leaving.)

Itte irasshai.
いって　いらっしゃい。

I hope you have a pleasant trip.
Have a good time.
(an expression used by a person saying goodbye to someone)

Lesson 11

imasu 　[kodomo ga～]	います 　[こどもが～]	have [a child]
imasu 　[Nihon ni～]	います 　[にほんに～]	stay, be [in Japan]
kakarimasu	かかります	take (referring to time)
hitotsu	ひとつ	one (when counting things)
futatsu	ふたつ	two
mittsu	みっつ	three
yottsu	よっつ	four
itsutsu	いつつ	five
muttsu	むっつ	six
nanatsu	ななつ	seven
yattsu	やっつ	eight
kokonotsu	ここのつ	nine
tō	とお	ten
ikutsu	いくつ	how many
hitori	ひとり	one person
futari	ふたり	two people
-nin	―にん	-people
-dai	―だい	(counter for machines, cars, etc.)
-mai	―まい	(counter for paper, stamps, etc.)
-kai	―かい	-times
kyōdai	きょうだい	brothers and sisters

kippu	きっぷ	ticket
fūtō	ふうとう	envelope
kitte	きって	postage stamp
ea-mēru	エアメール	airmail
nimotsu	にもつ	baggage, parcel
ichi-nichi（1-nichi） いちにち		one day (as a period of time)
-jikan	—じかん	-hour (s)
-shūkan	—しゅうかん	-week (s)
-kagetsu	—かげつ	-month (s)
-nen	—ねん	-year (s)
donokurai	どのくらい	how long, how many
～gurai	～ぐらい	about～ (referring to an amount or a period of time)
zenbu de	ぜんぶで	in total
～dake	～だけ	only～, exactly
sorekara	それから	and, then (the next thing), furthermore

Lesson 12

hima[na]	ひま[な]	free (time)
isogashii	いそがしい	busy
chikai	ちかい	near
tōi	とおい	far
hayai	はやい	fast, early
osoi	おそい	slow
ōi 　[hito ga~]	おおい 　[ひとが~]	many [people]
sukunai 　[hito ga~]	すくない 　[ひとが~]	few [people]
atatakai	あたたかい	warm
suzushii	すずしい	cool
amai	あまい	sweet
karai	からい	hot (taste), spicy
tanoshii	たのしい	enjoyable, pleasant
wakai	わかい	young
ii 　[kōhii ga~]	いい 　[コーヒーが~]	prefer [coffee]
tenki	てんき	weather, fine weather
ame	あめ	rain
yuki	ゆき	snow
kumori	くもり	cloudy
yasumi	やすみ	holiday, an absence
ryokō	りょこう	trip, tour
pātii	パーティー	party
mise	みせ	store, shop
kurasu	クラス	a class (a group of students)

24

dochira	どちら	which (to distinguish one thing from another, particularly when selecting one out of two)
dochira mo	どちらも	both
ichiban	いちばん	number one, the most～
totemo	とても	very
zutto	ずっと	far ～, much～ (comparing one thing with others)
demo	でも	but

*　　*　　*　　*　　*

Tadaima.
　ただいま。

I'm home. , Just now.
(used to announce one's return home)

Okaerinasai.
　おかえりなさい。

Welcome home！, Please return.
(said to someone who has just come home)

Tsukaremashita.
　つかれました。

(I'm) tired.

Lesson 13

asobimasu I (asobu, asonde)　　　　　　　　　enjoy oneself, play
あそびます（あそぶ、あそんで）

okurimasu [nimotsu o～] I (okuru, okutte)　　send[baggage, parcel]
おくります［にもつを～］（おくる、おくって）

kaemasu II (kaeru, kaete)　　　　　　　　　change
かえます（かえる、かえて）

kekkon-shimasu III (-suru, -shite)　　　　　get married
けっこんします（～する、～して）

kaimono-shimasu III (-suru, -shite)　　　　do shopping
かいものします（～する、～して）

sanpo-shimasu [kōen o～] III (-suru, -shite)　take a walk [in a park]
さんぽします［こうえんを～］（～する、～して）

kenbutsu-shimasu [machi o～] III (-suru, -shite) do sightseeing [in a town]
けんぶつします［まちを～］（～する、～して）

kengaku-shimasu [kōjō o～] III (-suru, -shite)　visit [a factory]
けんがくします［こうじょうを～］（～する、～して）

hairimasu [heya ni～] I (hairu, haitte)　　enter [the room]
はいります［へやに～］（はいる、はいって）

demasu [heya o～] II (deru, dete)　　　　go out [of the room]
でます［へやを～］（でる、でて）

hoshii　　　　　ほしい　　　　　　　　　want（something）

bideo	ビデオ	video cassette recorder, video tape
rajikase	ラジカセ	radio cassette tape recorder
sutereo	ステレオ	stereo
kuruma	くるま	vehicle
omiyage	おみやげ	souvenir, present
itsumo	いつも	always
tokidoki	ときどき	sometimes
dokoka	どこか	somewhere, some place
nanika	なにか	something

*   *   *   *   *

Ii tenki desu ne.
いい　てんきですね。

Nice weather, isn't it ?

Sō desu ne.
そうですね。

Yes, it is. , I agree.
(when making agreeable responses)

Onaka ga sukimashita.
おなかが　すきました。

(I'm) hungry.

Onaka ga ippai desu.
おなかが　いっぱいです。

(I'm) full.

Nodo ga kawakimashita.
のどが　かわきました。

(I'm) thirsty.

Sō shimashō.
そう　しましょう。

Let's do that.
(when agreeing with someone's suggestion)

Lesson 14

yobimasu I （yobu, yonde）　　　　　　call
よびます （よぶ、よんで）

isogimasu I （isogu, isoide）　　　　　hurry
いそぎます （いそぐ、いそいで）

machimasu I （matsu, matte）　　　　　wait
まちます （まつ、まって）

torimasu I （toru, totte）　　　　　　take
とります （とる、とって）

tetsudaimasu I （tetsudau, tetsudatte）　help (with a task)
てつだいます （てつだう、てつだって）

iimasu I （iu, itte）　　　　　　　　say
いいます （いう、いって）

hanashimasu I （hanasu, hanashite）　　speak
はなします （はなす、はなして）

oboemasu II （oboeru, oboete）　　　　remember, memorize
おぼえます （おぼえる、おぼえて）

oshiemasu II （oshieru, oshiete）　　　tell, teach
おしえます （おしえる、おしえて）

misemasu II （miseru, misete）　　　　show
みせます （みせる、みせて）

furimasu ［ame ga～] I （furu, futte）　rain
ふります ［あめが～] （ふる、ふって）

kotoba　　　　ことば　　　　　　　　word, language
namae　　　　なまえ　　　　　　　　name
jūsho　　　　　じゅうしょ　　　　　address
denwa-bangō　でんわばんごう　　　　telephone number
shio　　　　　しお　　　　　　　　　salt
satō　　　　　さとう　　　　　　　　sugar
kasa　　　　　かさ　　　　　　　　　umbrella

taipu	タイプ	typewriter, typewriting
wāpuro	ワープロ	word processor
tsukai-kata	つかいかた	method of use
kaki-kata	かきかた	method of writing
yomi-kata	よみかた	method of reading
yukkuri	ゆっくり	slowly
mō ichido	もう　いちど	one more time, once more
mata	また	again, next chance
mō sukoshi	もう　すこし	a little more
hayaku	はやく	fast, early
sugu	すぐ	immediately
ato de	あとで	later

*　　　*　　　*　　　*　　　*

【Yasui no】 wa arimasen ka.
　【やすいの】は　ありませんか。

Kochira wa ikaga desu ka.
　こちらは　いかがですか。

Ūn···
　ううん···

[Dōmo] sumimasen.
　[どうも]　すみません。

Mata kimasu.
　また　きます。

Do you have a 【cheap one】?

How about this one ?

Hmm...
(when wondering what to do)

I'm [very] sorry.
(an apology)

I'll come again.
(can be used as an excuse when leaving a shop without buying anything)

Lesson 15

tsukaimasu I （tsukau, tsukatte）
つかいます （つかう、つかって）

use

tsukemasu II （tsukeru, tsukete）
つけます （つける、つけて）

turn on (a light, etc.)

keshimasu I （kesu, keshite）
けします （けす、けして）

turn off (a light, etc.)

akemasu II （akeru, akete）
あけます （あける、あけて）

open

shimemasu II （shimeru, shimete）
しめます （しめる、しめて）

shut

suwarimasu [isu ni～] I （suwaru, suwatte）
すわります [いすに～] （すわる、すわって）

sit down [on a chair]

tachimasu I （tatsu, tatte）
たちます （たつ、たって）

stand up

okimasu I （oku, oite）
おきます （おく、おいて）

put

tsukurimasu I （tsukuru, tsukutte）
つくります （つくる、つくって）

make, produce

urimasu I （uru, utte）
うります （うる、うって）

sell

shirimasu I （shiru, shitte）
しります （しる、しって）

get to know

mochimasu I （motsu, motte）
もちます （もつ、もって）

hold

sumimasu I （sumu, sunde）
すみます （すむ、すんで）

be going to live

shitte imasu　しって　います

know

motte imasu　もって　います

be holding, have

sunde imasu　すんで　います
　[Tōkyō ni ～]　[とうきょうに～]

live [in Tokyo]

kin'en	きんえん	no smoking
seihin	せいひん	products
sekken	せっけん	soap
taoru	タオル	towel
dokushin	どくしん	single, unmarried
[o-]shigoto	[お] しごと	work, business
enjinia	エンジニア	engineer
kaishain	かいしゃいん	company employee
ginkōin	ぎんこういん	bank employee
gakusei	がくせい	student
daigaku	だいがく	university
ue no【imōto】	うえの【いもうと】	elder【younger sister】
shita no【imōto】	したの【いもうと】	younger【younger sister】
imōto-san	いもうとさん	(someone else's) younger sister

Lesson 16

arukimasu Ⅰ （aruku, aruite）   walk
あるきます （あるく、あるいて）

norimasu ［densha ni～］ Ⅰ （noru, notte）   get ［a train］
のります ［でんしゃに～］ （のる、のって）

orimasu ［densha o～］ Ⅱ （oriru, orite）   get off ［a train］
おります ［でんしゃを～］ （おりる、おりて）

norikaemasu Ⅱ （norikaeru, norikaete）   change ［trains］
のりかえます （のりかえる、のりかえて）

shokuji-shimasu Ⅲ （-suru, -shite）   have a meal, dine
しょくじします （～する、～して）

araimasu Ⅰ （arau, aratte）   wash
あらいます （あらう、あらって）

abimasu ［shawā o～］ Ⅱ （abiru, abite）   take ［a shower］
あびます ［シャワーを～］ （あびる、あびて）

nagai	ながい	long
mijikai	みじかい	short
omoi	おもい	heavy
karui	かるい	light
hiroi	ひろい	wide
semai	せまい	narrow, small (room)
akarui	あかるい	bright
kurai	くらい	dark
se ga takai	せが たかい	tall (referring to person)

karada	からだ	body
kao	かお	face
me	め	eye
hana	はな	nose
kuchi	くち	mouth
mimi	みみ	ear
ha	は	tooth
kami	かみ	hair
te	て	hand
ashi	あし	leg, foot

shawā	シャワー	shower
hanbāgu	ハンバーグ	hamburger
-ban	ーばん	number-
dono~	どの~	which~
dōyatte	どうやって	in what way, how
iroiro	いろいろ	various
~goro	~ごろ	about~, around~ (referring to time)

*   *   *   *   *

Nan demo ii desu.
なんでも　いいです。

Anything will be fine.

Nan ni shimasu ka.
なんに　しますか。

What would you like ?
(asking to choose something)

【Sore】 ni shimasu.
【それ】に　します。

I'll take 【that】.
(having made a choice)

Ēto···
ええと・・・

Uh, Hmm..., Let me see.
(used when pausing)

Lesson 17

wasuremasu Ⅱ （wasureru, wasurete）　　　forget
わすれます （わすれる、わすれて）

nakushimasu Ⅰ （nakusu, nakushite）　　　lose
なくします （なくす、なくして）

shinpai-shimasu Ⅲ （-suru, -shite）　　　worry
しんぱいします （～する、～して）

ki o tsukemasu [kuruma ni～] Ⅱ　　　pay attention to [a car]
（ki o tsukeru, ki o tsukete）
きを つけます [くるまに～] （きを つける、きを つけて）

iremasu Ⅱ （ireru, irete）　　　put in, insert
いれます （いれる、いれて）

dashimasu Ⅰ （dasu, dashite）　　　take out, hand in
だします （だす、だして）

tomemasu Ⅱ （tomeru, tomete）　　　stop, park (a car)
とめます （とめる、とめて）

kaeshimasu Ⅰ （kaesu, kaeshite）　　　give back, return
かえします （かえす、かえして）

haraimasu Ⅰ （harau, haratte）　　　pay
はらいます （はらう、はらって）

nugimasu Ⅰ （nugu, nuide）　　　take off (clothes, shoes, etc.)
ぬぎます （ぬぐ、ぬいで）

sawarimasu [kikai ni～] Ⅰ （sawaru, sawatte）　　　touch [a machine]
さわります [きかいに～] （さわる、さわって）

taisetsu[na]　　　たいせつ[な]　　　important, precious

sugoi　　　すごい　　　brilliant !, great !
(expresses astonishment
and admiration)

abunai　　　あぶない　　　dangerous

oto	おと		sound
robotto	ロボット		robot
kyoka	きょか		permission
suitchi	スイッチ		switch
kūrā	クーラー		air conditioner
hiitā	ヒーター		heater
maishū	まいしゅう		every week
～made ni	～までに		before～, by～ (indicating time limit)
desukara	ですから		therefore, so

          *   *   *   *   *

Dame desu.
だめです。   That's no good, You must not.

Zannen desu.
ざんねんです。   I'm sorry (to hear that).
                              That's a pity.

Lesson 18

dekimasu Ⅱ （dekiru, dekite）   can, be able to
できます（できる、できて）

utaimasu Ⅰ （utau, utatte）   sing
うたいます（うたう、うたって）

hikimasu [piano o～] Ⅰ （hiku, hiite）   play [the piano]
ひきます［ピアノを～］（ひく、ひいて）

oyogimasu Ⅰ （oyogu, oyoide）   swim
およぎます（およぐ、およいで）

naoshimasu Ⅰ （naosu, naoshite）   repair
なおします（なおす、なおして）

unten-shimasu Ⅲ （-suru, -shite）   drive
うんてんします（～する、～して）

renshū-shimasu Ⅲ （-suru, -shite）   practice
れんしゅうします（～する、～して）

hajimemasu Ⅱ （hajimeru, hajimete）   begin
はじめます（はじめる、はじめて）

kantan[na]   かんたん［な］   easy

koshō	こしょう	out of order, break down
shumi	しゅみ	hobby, pastime
e	え	picture, drawing
piano	ピアノ	piano
sukii	スキー	ski
-mētoru	ーメートル	-meter
doru	ドル	dollar

* * * * *

Daijōbu desu.
だいじょうぶです。

It's nothing to worry about. It's all right.

Mada mada dame desu.
まだまだ　だめです。

I'm still no good.
(an expression of modesty)

Motto 【renshū-shi】 nai to.
もっと【れんしゅうし】ないと。

I need more 【practice】.

Lesson 19

sōji-shimasu Ⅲ（-suru, -shite）   clean (a room)
　そうじします（～する、～して）

sentaku-shimasu Ⅲ（-suru, -shite）   wash (clothes)
　せんたくします（～する、～して）

dekakemasu Ⅱ（dekakeru, dekakete） go out (of a house)
　でかけます（でかける、でかけて）

tomarimasu [hoteru ni～] Ⅰ（tomaru, tomatte） stay [at a hotel]
　とまります［ホテルに～］（とまる、とまって）

narimasu Ⅰ（naru, natte）   become
　なります（なる、なって）

sukiyaki	すきやき	sukiyaki (meat and vegetable hotpot)
tenpura	てんぷら	tempura (seafood and vegetables fried in batter)
sashimi	さしみ	sashimi (raw fish)
sushi	すし	sushi (raw fish on vinegared rice)
kabuki	かぶき	Kabuki (Japanese classical drama)
gaikoku	がいこく	foreign country
hoteru	ホテル	hotel

ichido mo	いちども	not once, never (used in negative sentence)
zehi	ぜひ	by all means
hajimete	はじめて	for the first time
dandan	だんだん	gradually

*   *   *   *   *

Gomen kudasai.
ごめんください

Excuse me. , Anybody home ?, May I come in ? (an expression used by a visitor)

Sā
さあ

Come on ! , Why don't you ? (used when encouraging some one to do something)

Shitsurei-shimasu.
しつれいします。

Excuse me.

Sorosoro 【shitsurei-shimasu】.
そろそろ 【しつれいします】。

It's almost time 【to leave】 now. (used before leaving)

【Kyō 】 wa dōmo arigatō gozaimashita.
【きょう】は どうも ありがとう ございました。

Thank you very much for everything 【today】

Lesson 20

irimasu [jisho ga~] Ⅰ (iru, itte) いります [じしょが~] (いる、いって)		need [a dictionary]
boku	ぼく	I (an informal equivalent of "watashi" used by men)
kimi	きみ	you (an informal equivalent of "anata" used by men)
~kun	~くん	Mr. (an informal equivalent of "san" used for men)
un	うん	yes (an informal equivalent of "hai")
uun	ううん	no (an informal equivalent of "iie")
kotchi	こっち	this way (the informal form of "kochira")
sotchi	そっち	that way (the informal form of "sochira")
atchi	あっち	that way (the informal form of "achira")
dotchi	どっち	which way (the informal form of "dochira")
basho	ばしょ	place

*   *   *   *   *

Matte iru yo.
まって いるよ。

I'll be waiting for you.

Lesson 21

omoimasu I （omou, omotte）   think
おもいます（おもう、おもって）

yaku ni tachimasu I   be useful
（yaku ni tatsu, yaku ni tatte）
やくに たちます（やくに たつ、やくに たって）

benri [na]	べんり [な]	convenient, useful, handy
fuben [na]	ふべん [な]	inconvenient
onaji	おなじ	the same
kenshū-ryokō	けんしゅうりょこう	study trip
kaigi	かいぎ	meeting
shitsumon	しつもん	question
iken	いけん	opinion
gijutsu	ぎじゅつ	technology, engineering
kōtsū	こうつう	transportation
minna	みんな	all, everything
tabun	たぶん	probably
kitto	きっと	surely
hontō ni	ほんとうに	really
～ ni tsuite	～に ついて	about ～
hoka no～	ほかの～	another ～
keredomo	けれども	but

[Nihon wa] gijutsu ga susunde imasu.　　　[Japan] is technologically ad-
　[にほんは] ぎじゅつが　すすんで　います。　vanced.

Lesson 22

kimasu [shatsu o～] II （kiru, kite）   wear [a shirt, etc.]
きます [シャツを～] （きる、きて）

hakimasu [kutsu o～] I （haku, haite）   wear [shoes, trousers, etc.]
はきます [くつを～] （はく、はいて）

kaburimasu [bōshi o～] I [kaburu, kabutte]   wear [a hat, etc.]
かぶります [ぼうしを～] （かぶる、かぶって）

kakemasu [megane o～] II （kakeru, kakete）   wear [glasses, etc.]
かけます [めがねを～] （かける、かけて）

motte ikimasu I （motte iku, motte itte）   take （something）
もって いきます （もって いく、もって いって）

motte kimasu III （motte kuru, motte kite）   bring （something）
もって きます （もって くる、もって きて）

buhin	ぶひん	parts
herumetto	ヘルメット	helmet
fuku	ふく	dress, clothes
kōto	コート	coat
sētā	セーター	sweater
bōshi	ぼうし	hat
megane	めがね	glasses
yakusoku	やくそく	promise, appointment
mēkā	メーカー	manufacturer, maker

Mata kondo onegai-shimasu.
また　こんど　おねがいします。

Please ask me again some other time.
(refusing an invitation indirectly, considering someone's feelings)

Osaki ni [shitsurei-shimasu].
おさきに［しつれいします］。

Excuse me. (for leaving before you).
(used when leaving somewhere first)

Otsukaresama [deshita].
おつかれさま［でした］。

Thank you for your work.
(used when appreciating someone's work, but not used towards one's superiors)

45

Lesson 23

kikimasu [sensei ni ～] I （kiku, kiite）   ask [the teacher]
ききます [せんせいに～] （きく、きいて）

oshimasu I （osu, oshite）   push, press
おします （おす、おして）

mawashimasu I （mawasu, mawashite）   rotate, turn
まわします （まわす、まわして）

ugokimasu [kikai ga～] I （ugoku, ugoite）   [a machine] move, work
うごきます [きかいが～] （うごく、うごいて）

tomarimasu [kikai ga～] I （tomaru, tomatte）   [a machine] stop
とまります [きかいが～] （とまる、とまって）

demasu [kippu ga～] II （deru, dete）   [a ticket] come out
でます [きっぷが～] （でる、でて）

chōsetsu-shimasu III （-suru, -shite）   adjust
ちょうせつします （～する、～して）

komarimasu I （komaru, komatte）   have a problem
こまります （こまる、こまって）

ganbarimasu I （ganbaru, ganbatte）   do one's best
がんばります （がんばる、がんばって）

watarimasu [michi o～] I （wataru, watatte）   cross [a road]
わたります [みちを～] （わたる、わたって）

magarimasu [migi e～] I （magaru, magatte）   turn [right]
まがります [みぎへ～] （まがる、まがって）

kanashii   かなしい   sad

ureshii   うれしい   glad, happy

sabishii   さびしい   lonely

nemui   ねむい   sleepy

imi	いみ	meaning
otsuri	おつり	change
komakai okane	こまかい　おかね	small change
【sen-en】 satsu	【せんえん】 さつ	【1,000-yen】 note, bill
botan	ボタン	button
michi	みち	way, road
hashi	はし	bridge
shingō	しんごう	traffic lights
ima	いま	nowadays
massugu	まっすぐ	straight on
yoku	よく	often

*　*　*　*　*

Komatta na.
　こまったな。

Tch！tch！, Oh, my god！, What shall I do?

Nan ni tsukaimasu ka.
　なんに　つかいますか。

What is (this) for?

Lesson 24

kuremasu II (kureru, kurete)　　　　　give something (to me)
くれます（くれる、くれて）

setsumei-shimasu III (-suru, -shite)　　explain
せつめいします（〜する、〜して）

kopii-shimasu III (-suru, -shite)　　　make a photocopy
コピーします（〜する、〜して）

annai-shimasu III (-suru, -shite)　　　show around, show the
あんないします（〜する、〜して）　　way

shōkai-shimasu III (-suru, -shite)　　introduce
しょうかいします（〜する、〜して）

tsurete ikimasu I (tsurete iku, tsurete itte)　take (someone)
つれて　いきます（つれて　いく、つれて　いって）

tsurete kimasu III (tsurete kuru, tsurete kite)　bring (someone)
つれて　きます（つれて　くる、つれて　きて）

okurimasu [hito o〜] I (okuru, okutte)　　see (someone) home
おくります［ひとを〜］（おくる、おくって）

shirabemasu II (shiraberu, shirabete)　　check up, investigate
しらべます（しらべる、しらべて）

okashi　　　おかし　　　　　cake, candy, sweets
ningyō　　　にんぎょう　　　doll
meishi　　　めいし　　　　　name card, business card

Tōkyō-tawā	とうきょうタワー	Tokyo Tower
Ōsakajō	おおさかじょう	Osaka Castle
jibun de	じぶんで	by oneself
konoaida	このあいだ	the other day

* * * * *

Hontō desu ka.
ほんとうですか。

Is that true?

Ganbatte kudasai.
がんばって　ください。

Give it your best shot!
Good luck!
(a word of encouragement)

Lesson 25

kangaemasu II （kangaeru, kangaete）　　　　think
かんがえます（かんがえる、かんがえて）

tsuzukemasu II （tsuzukeru, tsuzukete）　　　continue
つづけます（つづける、つづけて）

yamemasu [benkyō o ～] II （yameru, yamete）　stop [studying], resign
やめます [べんきょうを～]（やめる、やめて）　（from one's company）

iremasu [suitchi o ～] II （ireru, irete）　　switch on
いれます [スイッチを～]（いれる、いれて）

kirimasu [suitchi o ～] I （kiru, kitte）　　switch off
きります [スイッチを～]（きる、きって）

katazukemasu II （katazukeru, katazukete）　put (things) in order
かたづけます（かたづける、かたづけて）　　　tidy up

naoshimasu [machigai o ～] I (naosu, naoshite)　correct [a mistake]
なおします [まちがいを～]（なおす、なおして）

machigai	まちがい	mistake
dōgu	どうぐ	tool, instrument
ippan-kenshū	いっぱんけんしゅう	general orientation
pikunikku	ピクニック	picnic
sekai	せかい	world
komatta koto	こまった　こと	trouble, problem
moshi [～tara]	もし [～たら]	if～
ikura [～te mo]	いくら [～ても]	however ～, even if ～
itsudemo	いつでも	anytime

                    *   *   *   *   *

[Iroiro] osewa ni narimashita.   Thank you for everything you
[いろいろ] おせわに なりました。   have done for me.
                                                  (an expression of gratitude for
                                                  anyone who has helped you.)

Dōzo o-genki de.   Best of luck.
どうぞ おげんきで。   (greetings used when expecting
                                                  a long parting)

Mata aimashō.   See you again.
また あいましょう。

PART II

Related vocabulary

1. Specialities

2. Jobs

3. Food

4. Dishes

5. Seasonings

6. Illness · Injury

7. Body

8. Family

9. Inside a room

10. In a training centre

11. In town

12. At a station

13. Roads · Traffic

1　Senmon　　せんもん　　Specialities

kensetsu	けんせつ	construction
seizō	せいぞう	manufacturing, production
kōzō	こうぞう	structure
sekkei	せっけい	design, plan
chūzō	ちゅうぞう	casting, founding
kanagata	かながた	metal mould
bankin	ばんきん	sheet metal
kakō	かこう	processing, industrial processes
yōsetsu	ようせつ	welding
tosō	とそう	painting, coating
kumitate	くみたて	assembly
kensa	けんさ	inspection
seibi	せいび	maintenance, keeping in order
bunseki	ぶんせき	analysis
sōsa	そうさ	operation, manipulation
hanbai	はんばい	sales, marketing
konpyūtā no sofutouea		computer software
コンピューターの　ソフトウエア		

seisan-kanri	せいさんかんり	production control
kōtei-kanri	こうていかんり	process control
hinshitsu-kanri	ひんしつかんり	quality control
zaiko-kanri	ざいこかんり	stock control
		inventory control
kōjō-kanri	こうじょうかんり	factory management

kensetsu

yōsetsu

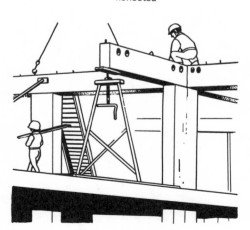

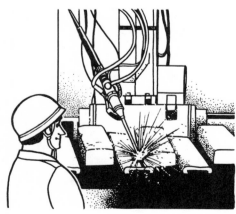

2 Shokugyō　　しょくぎょう　　Jobs

gijutsusha	ぎじゅつしゃ	engineer
kyōshi	きょうし	instructor
keikan	けいかん	policeman
isha	いしゃ	doctor
kangofu	かんごふ	nurse
tsūyaku	つうやく	interpreter
sarariiman	サラリーマン	salaried employee, white-collar worker
kōmuin	こうむいん	civil servant
shokuin	しょくいん	staff, personnel
jimuin	じむいん	office clerk
eki'in	えきいん	station employee
ten'in	てんいん	shop assistant
untenshu	うんてんしゅ	driver
shuei	しゅえい	guard, gatekeeper

gijutsusha

keikan

isha

3　Tabemono　たべもの　　Food

daikon	だいこん	Japanese radish
ninjin	にんじん	carrot
jagaimo	じゃがいも	potato
satsumaimo	さつまいも	sweet potato
mame	まめ	bean
kyūri	きゅうり	cucumber
hakusai	はくさい	chinese cabbage
kyabetsu	キャベツ	cabbage
negi	ねぎ	welsh onion, leek
tamanegi	たまねぎ	onion
nin'niku	にんにく	garlic
nira	にら	chinese chive, scallion
piiman	ピーマン	green pepper
moyashi	もやし	beansprouts
ichigo	いちご	strawberry
momo	もも	peach
nashi	なし	Japanese pear
kaki	かき	persimmon
suika	すいか	watermelon
budō	ぶどう	grape
maguro	まぐろ	tuna
aji	あじ	horse mackerel
sake	さけ	salmon
ebi	えび	shrimp, lobster, prawn
kai	かい	shellfish
ika	いか	cuttlefish, squid
tako	たこ	octopus

negi

piiman

ichigo

budō

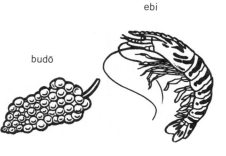

ebi

4 Ryōri　　りょうり　　　　Dishes

teishoku	ていしょく	set meal, table d'hôte
bentō	べんとう	boxed lunch
ranchi	ランチ	lunch
yaki-meshi (chāhan)	やきめし（チャーハン）	baked rice
gyūdon	ぎゅうどん	bowl of beef & rice
okayu	おかゆ	rice gruel
karē-raisu	カレーライス	rice with curry sauce
udon	うどん	(Japanese)noodles
soba	そば	buckwheat noodles
yaki-soba	やきそば	chow mein
rāmen	ラーメン	Chinese noodles
supagetti	スパゲッティ	spaghetti
yaki-niku	やきにく	grilled meat
yaki-zakana	やきざかな	grilled fish
medama-yaki	めだまやき	fried egg
yude-tamago	ゆでたまご	boiled egg
yasai-itame	やさいいため	stir-fried vegetables
ebi-furai	えびフライ	deep-fried prawns, scampi
tōsuto	トースト	toast
sandoitchi	サンドイッチ	sandwich
tsukemono	つけもの	pickled vegetables
sarada	サラダ	salad
misoshiru	みそしる	miso soup
sūpu	スープ	soup

bentō　　　yaki-zakana　　　medama-yaki

rāmen

yude-tamago

5 Chōmiryō　　ちょうみりょう　　Seasonings

shōyu	しょうゆ	soy sauce
sōsu	ソース	worcester sauce
miso	みそ	fermented soybean paste, miso
su	す	vinegar
abura	あぶら	oil
batā	バター	butter
mayonēzu	マヨネーズ	mayonnaise
kechappu	ケチャップ	ketchup
koshō	こしょう	pepper
tōgarashi	とうがらし	chilli, Cayenne pepper
shōga	しょうが	ginger
wasabi	わさび	Japanese horseradish
masutādo	マスタード	mustard
karē-ko	カレーこ	curry powder
shiokarai	しおからい	salty
suppai	すっぱい	sour
nigai	にがい	bitter
aji ga usui	あじが　うすい	lightly-seasoned, plain-tasting
aji ga koi	あじが　こい	lightly-seasoned, strongly-flavoured

shōyu

batā

tōgarashi

suppai

6 Byōki · kega びょうき・けが　　　Illness · Injury

arerugii	アレルギー	allergy
seki ga demasu	せきが　でます	have a cough
hanamizu ga demasu	はなみずが　でます	have a runny nose
chi ga demasu	ちが　でます	bleed
hakike ga shimasu	はきけが　します	feel nauseous
samuke ga shimasu	さむけが　します	feel chilled
geri o shimasu	げりを　します	have diarrhoea
benpi o shimasu	べんぴを　します	be constipated
kega o shimasu	けがを　します	get injured
yakedo o shimasu	やけどを　します	get burnt
shokuyoku ga arimasen		have no appetite
しょくよくが　ありません		
karada ga darui	からだが　だるい	feel tired and listless
kayui	かゆい	feel itchy
netsu o hakarimasu	ねつを　はかります	take one's temperature
kusuri o nurimasu	くすりを　ぬります	apply ointment
chūsha-shimasu	ちゅうしゃします	give an injection
shōdoku-shimasu	しょうどくします	disinfect, sterilize
nyō o torimasu	にょうを　とります	take a urine sample
taionkei	たいおんけい	clinical thermometer
bansōkō	ばんそうこう	sticking plaster
hōtai	ほうたい	bandage
gāze	ガーゼ	gauze
bandoeido	バンドエイド	Elastoplast, Band-Aid（sticking plaster）

59

kega o shimasu

netsu o hakarimasu

seki ga demasu

taionkei

yakedo o shimasu

7 Karada　　　からだ　　　Body

kubi	くび	neck
nodo	のど	throat
senaka	せなか	back
mune	むね	chest
hara	はら	belly
koshi	こし	waist
shiri	しり	buttocks
yubi	ゆび	finger
tsume	つめ	nail
ude	うで	arm
hiji	ひじ	elbow
hiza	ひざ	knee
i	い	stomach
chō	ちょう	bowels, intestines
hai	はい	lungs
shinzō	しんぞう	heart
kanzō	かんぞう	liver
jinzō	じんぞう	kidney

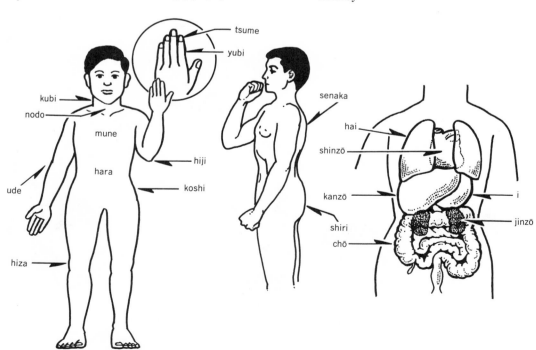

8 Kazoku   かぞく   Family

ryōshin	りょうしん	parents
chichi	ちち	(my)father
haha	はは	(my)mother
otto	おっと	(my)husband
tsuma	つま	(my)wife
ani	あに	(my)brother
ane	あね	(my)elder sister
sofu	そふ	(my)grandfather
sobo	そぼ	(my)grandmother
oji	おじ	(my)uncle
oba	おば	(my)aunt

chichi   haha

sofu   sobo

9 Heya no naka へやの　なか　　　　Inside a room

tenjō	てんじょう	ceiling
kabe	かべ	wall
yuka	ゆか	floor
tatami	たたみ	thick straw mat
jūtan	じゅうたん	carpet
oshi'ire	おしいれ	Japanese-style closet
tana	たな	shelf, shelves
kurōzetto	クローゼット	closet, cupboard
tansu	たんす	chest of drawers
kāten	カーテン	curtain
hikidashi	ひきだし	drawer
gomibako	ごみばこ	waste-paper basket
eakon	エアコン	air-conditioner
kotatsu	こたつ	low, quilted table with built-in heater
denki-sutando	でんきスタンド	desk lamp
konsento	コンセント	electrical outlet
futon	ふとん	Japanese-style bedding
makura	まくら	pillow
mōfu	もうふ	blanket
shiitsu	シーツ	sheet

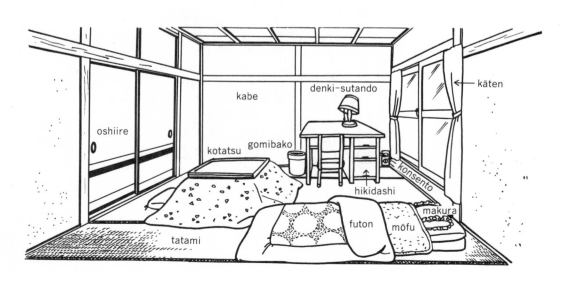

10   Sentā no naka センターの　なか   In a training centre

genkan	げんかん	front entrance
kaidan	かいだん	stairs
rōka	ろうか	corridor
ōsetsushitsu	おうせつしつ	reception room
toshoshitsu	としょしつ	library
shukuchokushitsu	しゅくちょくしつ	night duty room
chikashitsu	ちかしつ	basement
sentakushitsu	せんたくしつ	laundry room
sentakuki	せんたくき	washing machine
airon	アイロン	iron
[o-] furo	[お]ふろ	bath
beranda	ベランダ	verandah
okujō	おくじょう	roof
hijōguchi	ひじょうぐち	emergency exit
jidō-hanbaiki	じどうはんばいき	vending machine
shōkaki	しょうかき	fire extinguisher

11 Machi no naka まちの　なか   In town

kissaten	きっさてん	cafe, coffee shop
eigakan	えいがかん	cinema
hakubutsukan	はくぶつかん	museum
bijutsukan	びじゅつかん	art museum
dōbutsuen	どうぶつえん	zoo
shokubutsuen	しょくぶつえん	botanical garden
yūenchi	ゆうえんち	recreation ground, amusement park
otera	おてら	temple
jinja	じんじゃ	shrine
kyōkai	きょうかい	church
mosuku	モスク	mosque
shiyakusho	しやくしょ	city office
kuyakusho	くやくしょ	ward office
yakuba	やくば	public office
keisatsusho	けいさつしょ	police station
kōban	こうばん	police box
kōkō	こうこう	senior high school
chūgakkō	ちゅうがっこう	junior high school
shōgakkō	しょうがっこう	elementary school
yōchien	ようちえん	kindergarten
undōjō	うんどうじょう	playground, playing field
tai'ikukan	たいいくかん	gymnasium
pūru	プール	swimming pool

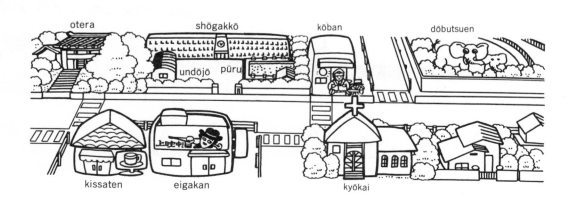

12 Eki えき At a station

kippu-uriba	きっぷうりば	ticket office
jidō-kenbaiki	じどうけんばいき	ticket machine
seisanjo	せいさんじょ	fare adjustment office
kaisatsuguchi	かいさつぐち	ticket gate
deguchi	でぐち	exit
iriguchi	いりぐち	entrance
higashi-guchi	ひがしぐち	east exit
nishi-guchi	にしぐち	west exit
minami-guchi	みなみぐち	south exit
kita-guchi	きたぐち	north exit
chūō-guchi	ちゅうおうぐち	central exit
(puratto)hōmu	(プラット)ホーム	platform
baiten	ばいてん	stall, kiosk
takushii-noriba	タクシーのりば	taxi stand
basu-tāminaru	バスターミナル	bus terminal
basutei	バスてい	bus stop
tokkyū	とっきゅう	limited express
kyūkō	きゅうこう	express
futsū	ふつう	ordinary, local
katamichi	かたみち	one-way, single
ōfuku	おうふく	return
jikokuhyō	じこくひょう	timetable
shuppatsu	しゅっぱつ	departure
tōchaku	とうちゃく	arrival
Tōkyō-iki	とうきょういき	bound for Tokyo

iriguchi   deguchi   baiten   jidō-kenbaiki   basutei

kaisatsuguchi

takushii-noriba

13 Dōro · kōtsū どうろ・こうつう Roads · Traffic

hodō	ほどう	pavement, sidewalk
shadō	しゃどう	roadway
kōsoku-dōro	こうそくどうろ	highway
tōri	とおり	street

kōsaten	こうさてん	crossroads
ōdan-hodō	おうだんほどう	pedestrian crossing
hodōkyō	ほどうきょう	footbridge
kado	かど	corner
【migi】gawa	【みぎ】がわ	【right】side
saka	さか	slope, hill
fumikiri	ふみきり	railway crossing
tonneru	トンネル	tunnel
chūshajō	ちゅうしゃじょう	car park
gasorin-sutando	ガソリンスタンド	petrol station
unten-menkyo	うんてんめんきょ	driving licence

66

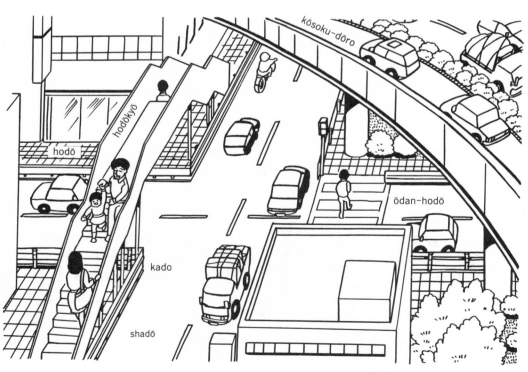

PART III

Translation

Sentence Patterns

Example Sentences

Conversation

Particles

How to use the Forms

**Adverbs,
Adverbial   Expressions**

Various Conjunctions

I Japanese pronunciation

1. Japanese syllables

2. Short vowels and long vowels

obasan (aunt)	:	obāsan (grandmother)
ojisan (uncle)	:	ojiisan (grandfather)
yuki (snow)	:	yūki (courage)
e (picture)	:	ē (yes)
heya (room)	:	heiya (plain)
koko (here)	:	kōkō (high school)
toru (take)	:	tōru (pass along)

3. Double consonants

oto (sound)	:	otto (husband)
kako (past)	:	kakko (parenthesis)
isai (details)	:	issai (one year old)

kippu (ticket), motto (more), match (matches)

4. Consonant + "ya, yu, yo"

hiyaku (leap, jump)	:	hyaku (one hundred)
riyū (reason)	:	ryū (dragon)
biyōin (beauty salon)	:	byōin (hospital)

kyaku (customer), nyūsu (news), ryokō (trip)

5. "za, zu, zo", and "ja, ju, jo"

zāzā (sound caused by a great amount of water, rain)

jājā (sound of water running.)

kazu (number)	:	kaju (fruit tree)
kōzō (strueture)	:	kōjō (factory)

6. "su" and "tsu"

isu (chair)	:	itsu (when)
suki (like)	:	tsuki (moon)
Suzuki (Mr. Suzuki)	:	tsuzuki (continuance)

tsukue (desk), atsui (hot), kyōshitsu (classroom)

II Classroom instructions and expressions

1. Let's begin.
2. Let's finish (the lesson).
3. Let's take a break.
4. Do you understand?
   ···Yes, I understand.
   ···No, I don't understand.
5. Once more.
6. Fine. Good.
7. No. No good.
8. name, room number
9. examination, homework
10. question, answer, example

III Greetings

1. Good morning.
2. Good affternon.
3. Good evening.
4. Good night.
5. Good bye.

IV Number

0 ···zero

1 ···one	6 ···six
2 ···two	7 ···seven
3 ···three	8 ···eight
4 ···four	9 ···nine
5 ···five	10···ten

Lesson 1

Sentence Patterns

1. I'm Rao.

2. Mr. Narong isn't Japanese.

3. Is Mr. Ali a trainee?

4. Mr. Lee is a trainee, too.

Example Sentences

1. Are you Mr.Rao?

   ···Yes, [I] am Rao.

   ···No, [I] am not Rao.

2. Is Mr. Narong Indonesian?

   ···No, [he] is not Indonesian. [He] is Thai.

3. Is Mr. Mario Thai, too?

   ···No, Mr. Mario is a Filipino.

4. Who is that?

   ···[He] is Mr. Rao.

5. Is Mr. Rao a trainee?

   ···Yes, [he] is a Tokyo Electric trainee.

6. How old is Mr. Tanaka?

   ···[He] is 28 [years old].

Conversation

Introducing each other

Tanaka : Good morning, everyone.

My name is Tanaka.

I'm happy to meet you.

Rao : How do you do?

I'm Rao, from India.

I'm a Tokyo Electric trainee.

My speciality is computer science.

Nice to meet you.

Lesson 2

Sentence Patterns

1. This is a book.
2. That is my book.
3. This book is mine.

Example Sentences

1. Is this a dictionary?

   ···Yes, it is.

2. Is that a pencil?

   ···No, it is not. [It] is a ballpoint pen.

3. What is that?

   ···[This] is a lighter.

4. Is that a ballpoint pen or a propelling pencil?

   ···[It] is a propelling pencil.

5. Whose bag is that?

   ···[That] is Mr. Lee's bag.

6. Is this dictionary yours?

   ···No, [it] is not mine.

7. Whose book is this?

   ···[It] is mine.

Conversation

At a reception desk

Rao   :   308, please.

Kimura :   Here you are.

            Is this your letter?

Rao   :   Yes, it is.

            Thank you very much.

Kimura :   Oh, wait a moment, please.

            Is this ballpoint pen yours, too?

Rao   :   No, it isn't.

Lesson 3

Sentence Patterns

1. This is a classroom.
2. The office is over there.

Example Sentences

1. Is this the reception desk?

   ···No, [it] is an office.

2. Where is the toilet?

   ···[It] is over there.

3. Where is Mr. Rao?

   ···[He] is in his room.

4. Which way (Where) is the dining hall?

   ···[It] is that way (over there).

5. What company are you with?

   ···[It] is NTC.

6. What kind of company is NTC?

   ···[It] is a computer company.

7. Where was that watch made?

   ···[It] is a Japanese one.

8. How much is this camera?

   ···[It] is 38,000 yen.

Conversation

At a department store

Rao	:	Excuse me.
Shop assistant A	:	Yes?
Rao	:	Where is the bag department?
Shop assistant A	:	The bag department? On the fifth floor.
Rao	:	Thank you.

Shop assistant B	:	May I help you?
Rao	:	How much is this bag?
Shop assistant B	:	It's 3,500 yen.
Rao	:	O.K., this one please.

Lesson 4

Sentence Patterns

1. It is ten past one.
2. I get up at six in the morning.
3. I work from nine to five.
4. I studied yesterday.

Example Sentences

1. What time is it now?

   ···[It] is five past four.

2. What time do you get up in the morning?

   ···[I] get up at six.

3. What time do you start and finish work every day?

   ···[I] work from eight o'clock to four o'clock.

4. What time does the lecture start?

   ···[It] starts at half past one.

5. Are you working tomorrow?

   ···Yes, [I] am going to work.

   ···No, [I] am not going to work.

6. Did you study last night?

   ···Yes, [I] did.

   ···No, [I] didn't study.

7. What day of the week is it today?

   ···[It] is Tuesday.

Conversation

Schedule

Kato : What time does the Japanese class begin?

Rao : It begins at nine o'clock.

Kato : What time does it end?

Rao : It ends at twelve o'clock.

Kato : I see.

What do you have in the afternoon?

Rao : I have a lecture.

Kato : What time does it finish?

Rao : It finishes at five o'clock.

Kato : You have a tough schedule every day, don't you?

Lesson 5

Sentence Patterns

1. I go to Kyoto. (I will go to Kyoto.)
2. I'm going home by air.
3. I came to Japan with a friend.

Example Sentences

1. Where will you go tomorrow?

   ···[I] will go to Kyoto.

2. Where did you go yesterday?

   ···[I] didn't go anywhere.

3. How do you get to Kyoto?

   ···[I] go [there] by Shinkansen.

4. Who did you come to the centre with?

   ···[I] came with Mr. Kato.

5. When did you come to Japan?

   ···[I] came in September.

   When will you return to your own country?

   ···[I] will return next year.

6. When (which month and which day) is your birthday?

   ···[My] birthday is March 15th.

Conversation

Taking a train

Rao   :   Excuse me. How much is it to Yokohama?

Woman: It is 300 yen.

Rao   :   Thank you.

Rao   :   Ah, Miss Kimura, where are you going?

Kimura: I'm going home. And you, Mr. Rao?

Rao   :   I'm going to my friend's house.

              Does this train go to Yokohama?

Kimura: No, it doesn't.

              [The Yokohama train] goes from Platform 3.

Rao   :   I see. Thank you.

Lesson 6

Sentence Patterns

1. I (will) drink coffee.

2. I (will) buy a shirt at the department store.

3. Won't you have lunch (dinner) with me?

4. Let's take a rest in the lobby.

Example Sentences

1. Do you smoke?

   ···No, [I] don't smoke.

2. What do you [usually] eat every morning?

   ···[I] eat bread and eggs.

3. What did you eat this morning?

   ···[I] didn't eat anything.

4. What did you do last night?

   ···[I] studied Japanese. Then I wrote a letter.

5. Where did you buy those shoes?

   ···[I] bought [them] at a department store.

6. Would you like to go to a department store with me?

   ···Yes, let's go.

Conversation

Going to see a film

Rao   :   Hello. Is that Miss Sato? It's Rao here.

Sato   :   Oh, Mr. Rao. Good evening.

Rao   :   Are you free tomorrow?

Sato   :   Yes.

Rao   :   Well, shall we go and see a film in Yokohama together?

Sato   :   That sounds fine. Where shall we meet?

Rao   :   Let's meet at Yokohama station at three o'clock.

Sato   :   O.K.

Rao   :   Well, see you tomorrow.

Lesson 7

Sentence Patterns

1. I eat with chopsticks.
2. I (will) give a watch to Mr. Lee.
3. I received a dictionary from Mr. Tanaka.

Example Sentences

1. What do you repair a radio with?

   ···[I] repair [it] with a screwdriver.

2. Do you write [your] reports in Japanese?

   ···No, I write them in English.

3. Who did you write a letter to?

   ···[I] wrote [one] to my family.

4. Who did you learn Japanese from?

   ···[I] learnt [it] from someone in my company.

5. Have you already had lunch?

   ···Yes, [I] have.

6. Have you already written the report for your company?

   ···No, [I] haven't. I am going to start writing it soon.

Conversation

Present

Ali   : Happy birthday, Mr.Lee.

           This is a present for you. Here you are.

Lee   : Oh, what is it?

Ali   : It is a shirt from Indonesia.

Lee   : Thank you very much.

Ali   : Not at all.

Tanaka: That's a nice shirt.

Lee   : You mean this one?

           Mr.Ali gave me this for my birthday.

Lesson 8

Sentence Patterns

1. Mr. Rao is kind.
2. Tokyo is large.
3. Mr. Rao is a kind person.
4. Tokyo is a big city.

Example Sentences

1. Is the centre quiet?
   ···Yes, [it] is quiet.
   ···No, [it] is not quiet.

2. Is Thailand hot now?
   ···Yes, [it] is very hot.
   ···No, [it] is not so hot.

3. Is that dictionary good?
   ···No, [it] is not so good.

4. How do you like Japanese food?
   ···[It] is delicious but expensive.

5. What kind of person is Miss Kimura?
   ···[She] is beautiful and very kind.

6. Which is Mr. Rao's bag?
   ···That black one is.

Conversation

Visiting a Training Centre

Kato : Hi! Mr. Rao. Long time no see.

How are you?

Rao : Fine, thank you.

This way, please.

Rao : Would you like some coffee?

Kato : Oh, thank you.

I'll have a cup.

Good coffee, isn't it?

How are your Japanese studies going?

Rao : Well, it is difficult but interesting.

Lesson 9

Sentence Patterns

1. I like apples.

2. I have a camera.

3. I will go to the hospital because I have a stomachache.

Example Sentences

1. Do you like beer?

   ···No, [I] don't like [it].

2. What sports do you like?

   ···I like tennis.

3. Is Mr. Ali good at singing?

   ···Yes, [he] is very good [at it].

4. Have you got any money?

   ···Yes, I have a little.

5. Can you understand Chinese characters?

   ···No, [I] can't understand [them] at all.

6. Where are you going tonight?

   ···I'm not going anywhere because I have a lot of homework.

7. Why were you away from the office?

   ···Because I had a temperature.

Conversation

Illness

Rao   : Mr. Tanaka.

Tanaka: Yes, what is it?

Rao   : Sorry, but could you give me some medicine?

Tanaka: What's the matter?

Rao   : I've caught a cold.

Tanaka: Have you got a temperature?

Rao   : Yes, a slight one.

Tanaka: O.K., let's go to the hospital.

Rao   : Oh, yes, please.

Lesson 10

Sentence Patterns

1. Mr. Tanaka is in the office.

2. There is a television set in the lobby.

3. Mr. Rao is in his room.

4. The book is on the desk.

Example Sentences

1. Who is in the lobby?

   ···Mr. Lee is.

2. Who is in the garden?

   ···Nobody is.

3. What is there on the desk?

   ···There is a bag.

4. What is there in the room?

   ···There are various things, like a bed, a desk and a chair.

5. Where is Mr. Tanaka now?

   ···[He] is in the dining hall.

6. Where is the bookshop?

   ···[It] is near the station. [It] is between the bank and the
   supermarket.

Conversation

Asking the way

Rao : Excuse me, but is there a post office near here?

Kimura: Yes, there is. It's in front of the station.

Rao : In front of the station?

Kimura: You don't know? O.K., I'll draw a map.

The station is here.

Rao : I see.

Kimura: There is a department store in front of the station.

The post office is next to it.

Rao : Thank you. I'll be off then.

Kimura: Bye for now.

Lesson 11

Sentence Patterns

1. [I] will buy three apples.
2. There are two computers.
3. Mr. Rao will stay in Japan for a year.

Example Sentences

1. How many desks are there in the classroom?
    ···There are seven.

2. How many members are there in your family?
    ···There are four.

3. How many children does Mr. Lee have?
    ···He has two.

4. Give me five 80 yen-stamps, please.
    ···Yes. That's 400 yen in all.

5. How many times do you listen to the tape every night?
    ···[I] listen [to it] twice.

6. How long did you study Japanese in your own country?
    ···[I] studied [it] for only three weeks.

7. How long does it take from Tokyo to Osaka by Shinkansen?
    ···[It] takes about three hours.

Conversation

At a post office

Rao   :   Excuse me.

               How much is it to send this letter to India?

Clerk :   It's 80 yen.

Rao   :   And this parcel too, please.

Clerk :   By air mail?

Rao   :   Yes.

Clerk :   It's 2,700 yen.

Rao   :   How long will it take?

Clerk :   It takes about one week.

Lesson 12

Sentence Patterns

1. [It] was rainy yesterday.
2. [It] was cold yesterday.
3. Tokyo is bigger than Osaka.
4. Mr. Narong is the youngest in the class.

Example Sentences

1. Were [you] free yesterday?

   ···Yes, [I] was free.

   ···No, [I] was not free.

2. Was the trip enjoyable?

   ···Yes, [it] was enjoyable.

   ···No, [it] was not enjoyable.

3. Was the weather good?

   ···No, [it] was not so good.

4. How was the film yesterday?

   ···[It] was very interesting.

5. Is India hotter than Japan?

   ···Yes, [it] is much hotter.

6. Which is faster, the Shinkansen or an airplane?

   ···An airplane is faster.

7. Which do you prefer, meat or fish?

   ···I like both.

8. What sport do you like best?

   ···I like soccer best.

Conversation

Travelling

Rao   : I'm back.

Kimura: Welcome back.

          How was your trip?

Rao   : It was fun, but I feel a bit tired.

Kimura: How was the weather?

Rao   : It was a little cold, but it was a very fine day.

Kimura: Which place did you like best?

Rao   : Let me see... I liked Kyoto best.

Lesson 13

Sentence Patterns

1. I want a camera.

2. I want to see a movie.

3. I (will) go to a department store to buy some shoes.

Example Sentences

1. What do [you] want most now?

   ···[I] want a car.

2. What do [you] want to buy?

   ···[I] want to buy a video set.

3. [I] want something to drink.

   ···So do I. What do [you] want to drink?

   [I] want to drink some beer.

4. Would you like to go to Shinjuku [with me] tonight?

   ···I'm tired, so [I] don't want to go anywhere.

5. Where will [you] go?

   ···[I] will go to Yokohama to see a film.

6. Do [you] always have a lecture in the afternoon?

   ···No, sometimes [I] visit a factory.

7. What will [you] go to Tokyo for?

   ···[I] will go to visit my friend at his house.

8. What training have you come to Japan for?

   ···[I] have come [here] for computer training.

Conversation

Going out

Han : Nice weather, isn't it?

Rao : Yes. I want to go somewhere.

Han : Shall we go and visit Yokohama Park?

Rao : That's a good idea.

Rao : It is a beautiful park, isn't it?

Han : Yes. ···Wow, it's already twelve o'clock.

Rao : I'm hungry. How about you?

Han : I'm thirsty.

Rao : Shall we go to that restaurant?

Han : Yes, let's do that.

Lesson 14

Sentence Patterns

1. Please lend [me] a dictionary.
2. Mr. Lee is watching TV.

Example Sentences

1. Do you understand?
   ···No, [I] don't. Please speak slowly.

2. Excuse me. Please pass me the ashtray.
   ···Here you are.

3. Please hurry, we're out of time.
   ···Just a moment. I'll be right there.

4. Do you know how to use a word processor?
   ···No, I don't. Please show me.

5. Please show me the tape recorders.
   ···What type of tape recorder do you want?
   Please show me some small ones.

6. What are you doing now?
   ···I am doing my homework.
   O.K., I'll come back later.

7. [It] is raining. Shall [I] call a taxi?
   ···Yes, please.

Conversation

At a camera shop

Shop assistant	:	May I help you?
Rao	:	Excuse me. Could you show me that camera?
Shop assistant	:	Certainly. Here you are.
Rao	:	It's a good camera, but it's too expensive.
		Don't you have a slightly cheaper one?
Shop assiatant	:	How about this one? It's 30,000 yen.
Rao	:	Hmm..., let me see.
		Sorry. Maybe some other time.

Lesson 15

Sentence Patterns

1. You may smoke.

2. Mr. Rao has a good camera.

Example Sentences

1. May [I] sit here?

   ···Yes, please do.

2. May [I] borrow this dictionary?

   ···[No,] I'm sorry. [I] am using [it] at the moment.

3. May [I] smoke here?

   ···No, [you] mustn't. This is a non-smoking area.

4. Where does Mr. Tanaka live?

   ···[He] lives in Tokyo.

5. Do [you] know the telephone number of the centre?

   ···No, [I] don't know.

6. Is Mr. Suzuki single?

   ···No, [he] is married.

7. What is [your] occupation?

   ···[I] am an engineer.

   [I] work for an automobile company.

Conversation

Family

Yamamoto:	Mr. Rao, are you married?
Rao :	No, I am single.
	I live with my family.
Yamamoto:	How many brothers and sisters do you have?
Rao :	I have two younger sisters.
Yamamoto:	How old are your younger sisters?
Rao :	The older one is twenty one years old.
	She works at a bank.
	The younger one is eighteen years old.
	She is studying at a university.

Lesson 16

Sentence Patterns

1. I get up in the morning, have breakfast, and go to the office.
2. After work, I go straight home.
3. Tokyo has a large population and is lively.

Example Sentences

1. What did [you] do yesterday?

   ···[I] went to a department store, did some shopping,
   and came back to the centre at about six o'clock.

2. How do [you] get to Yokohama Park?

   ···[You] go to Yokohama by train, take a No.80 bus
   and get off at "Kōen-mae".

3. After the lecture, what do [you] do?

   ···[I] play pingpong with my friends.

4. Which is Miss Han?

   ···She is that beautiful lady with long hair.

5. What kind of city is Kobe?

   ···[It] is a beautiful and lively city.

6. Who is that?

   ···That is Mr. Rao. [He] is Indian, and is a trainee
   at Tokyo Electric.

Conversation

Going to a restaurant

Kimura: After you finish studying, won't you eat out with me?

Narong: Yes, where shall we go?

Kimura: What would you like to eat, Mr. Narong?

Narong: Anything will do.

Kimura: Then I know an inexpensive and good restaurant.

Let's go there.

Kimura: What will you have?

Narong: Hmm...let's see.

Kimura: This restaurant does good hamburgers.

Narong: O.K., I'll have that.

Kimura: Excuse me. Two hamburgers, please.

Lesson 17

Sentence Patterns

1. Please don't take photographs.
2. I have to study every day.
3. I don't need to study on Saturday afternoons.

Example Sentences

1. [It] is dangerous, so please don't touch this machine.
   ···[I] see. [I] will be careful.

2. Shall [I] put some sugar in [your] coffee?
   ···No, thank you.

3. Do the factory workers understand English?
   ···No, they don't understand.
   So [I] must speak in Japanese.

4. By what time do [you] have to return to the centre?
   ···[I] must be back by twelve o'clock.

5. Must [I] submit a report every day?
   ···No, [you] don't have to submit [one] every day.
   Please submit [one] every Friday.

Conversation

Factory visit

Tanaka : Please don't touch the machines and products
in the factory.

Rao : I understand.

Rao : Wow! What a noise!
Mr. Tanaka, may I take a photo of that robot?

Tanaka : No, you can't.
You have to get permission.

Rao : I see. What a pity.

Lesson 18

Sentence Patterns

1. Mr.Lee can read Chinese characters.
2. My hobby is watching films.
3. I read a book before I go to bed.

Example Sentences

1. Can [you] ski?

   ···Yes, [I] can. But [I] am not very good [at it].

2. Can [you] play the guitar?

   ···No, [I] can't.

3. Can [I] change dollars into yen at the reception desk?

   ···No, [you] can't. Please go to a bank.

4. What is [your] hobby?

   ···[My hobby] is listening to music.

5. Did [you] study Japanese before [you] came to Japan?

   ···No, [I] did not study it at all.

   [I] started [studying it] after coming to Japan.

6. Please come to the office before the lecture.

   ···Yes, all right.

7. When did [you] get married?

   ···I got married three years ago.

Conversation

Skiing

Kimura : Would you like to go skiing next week?

Rao : I'd like to, but I can't ski.

Kimura : That's all right. It's easy.

Rao : You're good at skiing, aren't you, Miss Kimura?

Kimura : You're good too, Mr. Rao.

Rao : No, I'm still no good.

I need to practice more....

Kimura : O.K., let's practice a little more before we have lunch.

Lesson 19

Sentence Patterns

1. I have had Japanese food before.

2. On Sundays, I go shopping, see a film and so on.

3. From now on, it will get colder and colder.

Example Sentences

1. Have [you] ever been to Indonesia?

    ···Yes, [I] have. [I] went [there] with my friend three years ago.

2. Have [you] ever seen Mt. Fuji?

    ···No, never. [I] want to see [it] by all means.

3. What do [you] do at the centre every day?

    ···[We] study Japanese, attend lectures and so on.

4. Did [you] go anywhere on Sunday?

    ···No, [I] read some books and wrote some letters at home.

5. [It] has got dark, hasn't it? Shall [I] turn on the light?

    ···Yes, please.

6. How is [your] father's illness?

    ···[He] has already got better.

Conversation

Visit

Narong	:	Hello. Anybody home?
Yamamoto	:	Hey! Hello there! Come on in.
Narong	:	Thank you.

Mrs. Yamamoto	:	This is sukiyaki. Have you had it before?
Narong	:	No, I haven't. This is my first try.
Mrs. Yamamoto	:	Really? It's very good!
		Please help yourself.

Narong	:	Gosh, it's already nine o'clock.
		I must be going soon.
		Thank you very much for everything today.

Lesson 20

Sentence Patterns

1. [I] am going to Tokyo tomorrow.

2. [I] am busy every day.

3. It's nice weather today.

Example Sentences

1. Will [you] have some coffee?

   ···Yes, [I] will

   ···No, thank you.

2. Is there a television in your room?

   ···No, there isn't.

3. What did [you] buy at the department store?

   ···[I] didn't buy anything.

4. Would [you] like to have dinner (lunch) with me?

   ···Yes, that sounds nice.

5. How do you like Japanese food?

   ···[It] is delicious.

6. Are [you] free tomorrow?

   ···Yes, [I] am.

7. How was yesterday's examination?

   ···[It] was difficult.

8. Can [you] write Chinese characters?

   ···No, [I] can't.

9. Can I borrow a pair of scissors, please?

   ···Sure. But I need them too, so please give them back
   when you've finished with them.

Conversation

Party

Tanaka	:	Hello. Is that Mr. Hayashi's house?
Hayashi's brother	:	Yes, it is.
Tanaka	:	This is Tanaka. May I talk to Ichiro?

Tanaka	:	Mr. Hayashi? Are you free tomorrow evening?
Hayashi	:	Yes, I am. Why?
Tanaka	:	Like to go to a party?
Hayashi	:	Sounds great. Where is it?
Tanaka	:	At the Fuji Hotel.
		I'll be waiting for you in the lobby at six o'clock.
Hayashi	:	Got you. Till tomorrow, then.

Lesson 21

Sentence Patterns

1. I think it will rain tonight.

2. Someone from the company's said he would come to the centre tomorrow.

Example Sentences

1. Where is the key?

   ···[I] think [it] is in that bag.

2. Is anyone from your company coming to the party?

   ···No, [I] don't think [anyone] will come.

3. Is Mr. Tanaka in the office?

   ···[I] think [he] has already gone home,

   since his bag isn't [here].

4. How do you like [factory] visits?

   ···[They] are interesting,

   but [I] think the Q&A sessions are too short.

5. What do [you] think about Japan?

   ···[I] think that public transport is convenient.

6. In the meeting yesterday, [we] talked about factory visits.

   ···Did you? Did you give your opinion, too?

   Yes. [I] said that all the visits were good.

7. There's a party at the centre on Saturday, isn't there?

   ···Yes, there is.

Conversation

Meeting

Tanaka: Do you have anything to say about (factory) visits?

Narong: All the visits were good.

Rao : I think so, too.
I think Japanese technology is really advanced.

Tanaka: What kind of factories would you like to visit next time?

Narong: I'd like to visit some slightly smaller factories.

Tanaka: I see. How about everyone else?

Others : We have the same opinion.

Lesson 22

Sentence Patterns

1. This is a picture I took.
2. The man over there is Mr.Lee.

Example Sentences

1. Where did [you] buy this camera?

   ···[It] is the camera [I] bought in Shinjuku.

2. Who painted this picture? It's very good.

   ···[It] is the picture that Mr.Lee painted.

3. Who is that person wearing glasses?

   ···That's Mr.Tanaka.

4. Where did you visit last week?

   ···Nagoya Automobile Ltd.

5. How was the film [you] saw yesterday?

   ···[It] was very amusing.

6. What did [you] do yesterday afternoon?

   ···[I] visited a factory which makes auto parts.

7. Would you like to go out somewhere with me on Sunday?

   ···I'm sorry. [I] have arranged to meet a friend.

Conversation

After work

Tanaka : Won't you have dinner with me tonight. Mrs.Suzuki?

Suzuki : Yes, that would be nice.

Tanaka : How about joining us, Miss kimura?

Kimura : I'm sorry. I have arranged to meet a friend tonight.

Let me join you next time.

Tanaka : I see. That's too bad.

Kimura : Well, see you tomorrow. Goodbye.

(Excuse me for leaving earlier.)

Tanaka : Goodbye. (Thank you for your hard work.)

Lesson 23

Sentence Patterns

1. When you go abroad, you need a passport.
2. If you press this button, the machine will start.

Example Sentences

1. When [you] go to work, how do [you] usually go?
    ···[I] go by bus.

2. When [you] have no money, what do [you] do?
    ···[I] borrow [some] from a friend.

3. When did [you] take this picture?
    ···[I] took [it] when [I] went to Tokyo last week.

4. Until what time do [you] work?
    ···[I work] until five o'clock.
    But when [we] are busy, [I] work until about ten.

5. When [you] are free, what do you do?
    ···[I] watch TV, read books, and so on.

6. Do [you] often go skiing?
    ···No, [I] used to go often when [I] was a student,
    but these days [I] don't go very often.

7. How do [you] adjust the volume?
    ···You adjust [it] by turning this.

8. If [you] don't understand Japanese, [you] will have problems
    at the factory.
    ···I know. [I] will study hard.

9. Where is the station?
    ···Go straight down this street, and [you] will find it on your
    right.

Conversation

At a ticket vending machine

Rao : How much is it to Shinjuku?

Sato : It's 230 yen.

Rao : What shall I do? I don't have any small change.

Sato : No problem.
Put a 1,000-yen note in here, press the 230-yen button,
and the ticket and change will come out.

Rao : What is this button used for?

Sato : You use it when you buy two identical tickets.

Lesson 24

Sentence Patterns

    1.   Miss Kimura gave me a tie.

    2.   I lent Miss Kimura an umbrella.

    3.   I was taught Japanese by Mrs. Suzuki.

    4.   My wife sent me some photographs of my children.

Example Sentences

    1.   That's a nice tie.

         ···This one? My wife gave it to me.

         She always gives me a present on my birthday.

    2.   That's a beautiful shirt. Where is it from?

         ···It's an Indonesian shirt. Mr. Ali gave it to me the other day.

    3.   It's raining, isn't it? I didn't bring my umbrella.

         ···Well, shall I lend you mine?

         Yes, please.

    4.   I'm going to Yokohama Park tomorrow.

         ···Are you? Do you know the way?

         Yes, Miss Kimura told me.

    5.   I'm going to a factory in Nagoya tomorrow for technical training

         ···Are you? Who is going to take you?

         Mr. Takahashi is going with me.

Conversation

Studying Japanese

Hayashi : How long have you been studying Japanese?

Rao : I was taught it by a person in my company for about two weeks in India. After that, I studied it at the training centre for five weeks.

Hayashi : Really? You are so good at it.
Did you study hiragana and katakana too?

Rao : No. I want to study them by myself from now on.

Hayashi : Do you? Well, I have a good book, so I'll lend it to you. Study hard.

Lesson 25

Sentence Patterns

1. If it rains, I won't go.
2. Even if it rains, I will go.

Example Sentences

1. [There's a] picnic on Sunday,isn't there?

   If it rains, what will [you] do?

   ···If it rains, [I] won't go.

2. What shall we do if the bus doesn't come?

   ···Let's go by taxi.

3. [They] sell good video cassette recorders at that shop.

   ···Do they? [I] want to buy [some] if [they] are cheap.

4. If [you] are free tomorrow, shall [we] go to Tokyo Tower?

   ···Good idea. Let's go there.

5. When are [we] going to leave for the factory visit?

   ···[We] will leave immediately after having lunch.

6. The machine does not work.

   ···Did [you] turn the switch on?

   Yes, but [it] doesn't work even though [I] turned the switch on.

7. This radio cassette recorder is very expensive, isn't it?

   ···Yes, but [I] want to buy [it] however much it costs.

Conversation

After the Orientation

Tanaka : Your practical training starts next week, doesn't it?

Rao : Yes.

Tanaka : Please keep studying Japanese even after you go to the company.

Rao : Yes, I will.

Tanaka : Please write to me any time you have a problem.

Rao : Yes, I will. Thank you for all your help.
Thank you very much indeed.

Tanaka : O.K., best of luck. See you again.

Particles

1. **[wa]**

A: 1) My name is Rao.   (Lesson 1)

    2) This train is bound for Tokyo.   (5)

B: 1) We have a lecture in the afternoon.   (4)

    2) Would you like to eat out tonight?

       ···I have arranged to meet a friend.   (22)

2. **[mo]**

A: 1) He is a trainee. I am also a trainee.   (1)

    2) Give me two stamps. And an envelope, too.   (11)

    3) Which do you prefer, apples or oranges?

       ···I like both.   (12)

B: 1) I'm not going anywhere tomorrow.   (5)

    2) I didn't have anything to eat this morning.   (6)

    3) There's nobody in the garden.   (10)

120

3. **[no]**

A: 1) I'm Rao, from India.   (1)

    2) I'm a trainee at Tokyo Electric.   (1)

    3) This is my book.   (2)

    4) This is a watch made in Japan.   (3)

    5) NTC is a computer company.   (3)

B: 1) The Japanese lesson starts at nine.   (4)

    2) Will you teach me how to use a typewriter?   (14)

C: 1) Did you study last night?   (4)

    2) There is a book on the desk.   (10)

D: 1) This book belongs to me.   (2)

    2) Show me the small one.   (14)

4. **[o]**

A: 1) I have a meal.   (6)

    2) I play table tennis with my friends.   (6)

    3) I take my wife to Japan.   (24)

B: I take time off work.   (9)

C: 1) I go out of the room. (13)

   2) I get off the train. (16)

D: 1) I walk in the park. (13)

   2) I cross the bridge. (23)

   3) Walk straight down this road and you will reach the station. (23)

5. [ga]

A: 1) I like apples. (9)

   2) Mr. Ali is good at singing. (9)

   3) I have a camera. (9)

   4) I understand Japanese. (9)

   5) I have two children. (11)

   6) I want a camera. (13)

   7) I can ski. (18)

   8) I need a tape recorder. (20)

B: 1) I have a headache. (9)

   2) Miss Han has long hair. (16)

   3) Public transport is convenient in Japan. (21)

C: 1) There is a man. (10)

   2) There is a bank. (10)

   3) We will have a party at the centre tomorrow. (21)

D: 1) Which is faster, the Shinkansen or an airplane?

     ···An airplane is faster. (12)

   2) Mr. Narong is the youngest in the class. (12)

E: 1) It's raining now. (14)

   2) I go home immediately after work. (16)

   3) Press this button and the machine will stop. (23)

F: 1) This is a picture I took. (22)

   2) I want to take my family to Kyoto when they come to Japan. (25)

G: Mr. Ali gave me this shirt. (24)

6. [ni]

A: 1) I wake up at six every morning. (4)

   2) I arrived in Japan on September 15. (5)

B: 1) I gave my friend a book. (7)

   2) I call my workshop. (7)

C: 1) I received a watch from Mr. Kato. (7)

   2) I learnt Japanese from Mrs. Suzuki. (7)

D: 1) Mr. Tanaka is in the office. (10)

   2) The department store is in front of the station. (10)

   3) I live in Tokyo. (15)

E: 1) I enter the room. (13)

   2) May I sit on this chair? (15)

   3) I ride on a train. (16)

   4) You may not touch this machine. (17)

F: I go skiing. (18)

G: 1) I change dollars into yen. (18)

   2) Mr. Lee became ill. (19)

7. [e]

   1) I go to Kyoto. (5)

   2) I go to the department store for shopping. (13)

   3) Turn right and you will see a bank. (23)

8. [de]

A: 1) I go to Tokyo by train. (5)

   2) I repair a car with a screwdriver. (7)

   3) I write a report in Japanese. (7)

B: 1) I buy a shirt at a department store. (6)

C: Soccer is my favorite sport. (12)

9. [to]

A: 1) I go to Tokyo with my friend. (5)

   2) Mr. Rao is talking with the company representative. (14)

B: 1) I eat bread and eggs. (6)

   2) The bookshop is between the bank and the supermarket. (10)

C: Which do you prefer, coffee or tea? (12)

10. [ya]

   There's a bed, a desk, and chair in the room. (10)

11. **[kara] [made]**

    1) I work every day from 9 to 5. (4)

    2) The Japanese lesson starts at 9 o'clock. (4)

    3) The department store is open until 7. (4)

    4) The Shinkansen takes about three hours from Tokyo to Osaka. (11)

12. **[made ni]**

    You must return to the centre by 12. (17)

13. **[ka]**

    A: 1) Are you Mr. Rao? (1)

       2) Is that a ballpoint pen or a propelling pencil? (2)

       3) Won't you eat with me? (6)

    B: 1) Where is the bag department?

          ···The bag department? It's on the fifth floor. (3)

       2) The Japanese lesson starts at 9.

          ···I see. (4)

14. **[yori]**

    It is hotter in India than in Japan. (12)

15. **[ne]**

    1) I study from 9 to 5.

       ···Really? You work hard, don't you? (4)

    2) How about going to a film together?

       ···That sounds nice. (6)

    3) How are your Japanese studies?

       ···Well, it is difficult but interesting. (8)

16. **[yo]**

    Does this train go to Yokohama?

    ···No, it doesn't. The Yokohama train goes from platform 3. (5)

How to use the forms

1. **[masu-form]**

masu-form + mashō	Let's take a rest in the lobby. (Lesson 6)
masu-form + masen ka	Would you like to go to a department store with me? (6)
masu-form + tai desu	I want something to eat. (13)
masu-form + ni ikimasu	I'm going to Shinjuku to buy a camera. (13)
masu-form + mashō ka	Shall I call a taxi? (14)

2. **[te-form]**

te-form + kudasai	Excuse me, but could I borrow a dictionary? (14)
te-form + imasu	It is raining now. (14)
	I have a camera. (15)
te-form + mo ii desu	Do you mind my smoking? (15)
te-form + kara,~	I go home right after work. (16)
te-form, te-form,~	After waking up, I have breakfast and go to work. (16)
te-form + agemasu	I will lend you my umbrella. (24)
te-form + moraimasu	I learnt Japanese from Mrs. Suzuki. (24)
te-form + kuremasu	My wife sent me some photographs. (24)

3. **[nai-form]**

nai-form + nai de kudasai	Please refrain from taking pictures inside the factory. (17)
nai-form + nakereba narimasen	You must return to the centre by twelve. (17)
nai-form + nakute mo ii desu	You don't have to submit a report every day. (17)

4. **[dictionary-form]**

dic.-form + koto ga dekimasu	I can speak Japanese. (18)
dic.-form + koto desu	My hobby is watching films. (18)
dic.-form + mae ni,~	I usually take a shower before having dinner. (18)

124

5. **[ta-form]**

    ta-form + koto ga arimasu   I have been to Kyoto.   (19)

    ta-form + ri, **ta-form** + ri shimasu On Sundays, I wash clothes and clean my room. (19)

6. **[plain-form]**

    plain-form + to omoimasu   I am afraid it will rain tomorrow.   (21)

    I think prices in Japan are high.   (21)

    I think public transport in Japan is convenient. (21)

    plain-form + to iimasu   Mr. Kato said that he would visit the centre tomorrow.   (21)

    verb / **i-adjective** } **plain-form** } + deshō?

    na-adjective | **plain-form** ~ da

    noun

    There's a party at the centre on Saturday, isn't there? (21)

    Mt. Fuji is beautiful, isn't it?   (21)

    verb plain-form + **noun**   This photograph was taken by Mr. Tanaka. (22)

    The man with the hat is Mr. Ali.   (22)

7. **verb plain-form** / **i-adjectivei** ~i / **na-adjective** ~na / **noun** ~no } + toki, ~

    You need a passport when going abroad.   (23)

    I put a sweater on when I am feeling cold.   (23)

    I watch television when I am free.   (23)

    I often went skiing when I was a student.   (23)

8. **plain-form past** + ra, ~

    I won't go on the picnic if it rains tomorrow.   (25)

    I want to buy a camera if it's cheap.   (25)

    I'll go out if it's fine tomorrow.   (25)

9. **verb te-form** / **i-adjective** ~kute / **na-adjective** } ~de / **noun** } + mo, ~

    The machine doesn't start even though the switch is on.   (25)

    I want to buy a car however expensive it is.   (25)

    I'll go on the tour even if it rains.   (25)

10. **dic.-form** / **nai-form** } + to, ~

    Press this button and the machine will start.   (23)

    You will have trouble at the factory, if you don't understand Japanese.   (23)

Adverbs, Adverbial Expressions

1. **takusan**   Mr. Lee has a lot of money.   (Lesson 9)

    minna   All the factory visits were interesting.   (21)

    iroiro   I discussed various topics with my friend.   (16)

    taihen   It is very hot now in India.   (8)

    totemo   It is very fine today.   (12)

    yoku   Miss Han understands Japanese very well.   (9)

    daitai   I learned hiragana for three weeks,

                     and I can read almost all of them.   (9)

    sukoshi   I can understand English a little.   (9)

    chotto   Wait a moment.   (2)

    mō sukoshi   This camera is expensive.

                     Do you have a slightly cheaper one?   (14)

    zutto   India is far larger than Japan.   (12)

    ichiban   Apples are my favorite fruit.   (12)

126

2. **itsumo**   I always study Japanese in the morning.   (13)

    tokidoki   I sometimes visit a factory in the afternoon.   (13)

    yoku   I often went skiing when I was a student.   (23)

    hajimete   I have never been to Japan. This is my first visit.   (19)

    mō ichido   I beg your pardon. Once again, please.   (14)

    mata   See you again tomorrow.   (14)

3. **ima**   It is now one-thirty.   (4)

                     I often went skiing when I was a student,

                     but I seldom go now.   (23)

    sugu   I go home right after work.   (14)

    mō   Have you already had lunch?   (7)

    mada   No, I haven't.   (7)

    sorosoro   It is nine now. It is almost time for me to leave.   (19)

korekara	I'm going to have lunch.	(7)
ato de	Sorry. I'm busy now. Come and see me later.	(14)
konoaida	I went to Tokyo Tower the other day.	(24)

4.
issho ni	Won't you come to a department store with me?	(6)
hitori de	I came to Japan alone.	(5)
jibun de	I am going to study Hiragana by myself.	(24)
zenbu de	In all, there are five in my family.	(11)

hayaku	Please come to the classroom quickly.	(14)
yukkuri	Excuse me, but could you speak slowly?	(14)
dandan	It is getting colder and colder.	(19)
massugu	Go straight down this road,	
	and you will see the factory on your right.	(23)

5.
amari	This dictionary is not very practical.	(8)
zenzen	I cannot understand Chinese characters at all.	(9)
ichido mo	I have never tried Japanese food.	(19)
kitto	I am sure my family are all fine.	(21)
tabun	I think it will probably rain tomorrow.	(21)
moshi	I would like to buy a car if I had a lot of money.	(25)
ikura	I cannot understand its meaning,	
	however hard I search the dictionary.	(25)
zehi	I want so badly to ride on the Shinkansen,	
	as I have never tried it.	(19)

6.
mochiron	Mr. Lee is Chinese,	
	so of course he understands Chinese characters.	(9)
hontō ni	I think Mt. Fuji is really beautiful.	(21)

Various Conjunctions

1. **soshite**   Miss. Kimura is pretty, and she is also kind.   (Lesson 8)
   ~ de   Miss. Kimura is pretty and kind.   (16)
   ~ kute   The food served by that restaurant is inexpensive and good.   (16)
   sorekara   Give me some stamps. And I want to send this package too, please. (11)
   ~ tari   On Sundays, I go shopping, watch a movie and so on.   (19)
   ~ ga   Hello, this is Tanaka. Is Ichiro there?   (20)

2. **sorekara**   I'm going to have dinner, then I'm going to watch television.   (6)
   ~ te kara   After having dinner, I'll watch television.   (16)
   ~ te, ~ te,   I'll have dinner and watch television, then study Japanese.   (16)
   ~ mae ni   I study Japanese before I go to sleep.   (18)
   ~ toki   I always take the train when I commute to the office.   (23)

3. **~ kara**   I'm not going anywhere, as I have a lot of homework to do.   (9)
   desukara   The people at the factory don't understand English.
                     That's why you are required to speak Japanese.   (17)

4. **~ ga**   Japanese food tastes good, but it is expensive.   (8)
   demo   I want a camera, but I have no money.   (12)
   keredomo   Factory visits are interesting.
                     However, I think the time allowed for questions is too short.   (21)

5. **ja**   A: The price of this bag is 3,500 yen.
                     B: Then I'll take it.   (2)
   ~ to   Walk straight down this road,
                     and you'll see a factory on your right.   (23)
   ~ tara   I'll stay at home if it rains tomorrow.   (25)

6. **~ te mo**   I'll take a trip even if it rains.   (25)

PART IV

Appendices

1. Numerals

0	zero, rei	ゼロ、れい		100	hyaku	ひゃく
1	ichi	いち		200	ni-hyaku	にひゃく
2	ni	に		300	san-byaku	さんびゃく
3	san	さん		400	yon-hyaku	よんひゃく
4	yon, shi	よん、し		500	go-hyaku	ごひゃく
5	go	ご		600	rop-pyaku	ろっぴゃく
6	roku	ろく		700	nana-hyaku	ななひゃく
7	nana, shichi	なな、しち		800	hap-pyaku	はっぴゃく
8	hachi	はち		900	kyū-hyaku	きゅうひゃく
9	kyū, ku	きゅう、く				
10	jū	じゅう		1,000	sen	せん
11	jū ichi	じゅういち		2,000	ni-sen	にせん
12	jū ni	じゅうに		3,000	san-zen	さんぜん
13	jū san	じゅうさん		4,000	yon-sen	よんせん
14	jū yon	じゅうよん		5,000	go-sen	ごせん
	jū shi	じゅうし		6,000	roku-sen	ろくせん
15	jū go	じゅうご		7,000	nana-sen	ななせん
16	jū roku	じゅうろく		8,000	has-sen	はっせん
17	jū nana	じゅうなな		9,000	kyū-sen	きゅうせん
	jū shichi	じゅうしち				
18	jū hachi	じゅうはち		10,000	ichi-man	いちまん
19	jū kyū	じゅうきゅう		100,000	jū-man	じゅうまん
	jū ku	じゅうく		1,000,000	hyaku-man	ひゃくまん
20	ni-jū	にじゅう		10,000,000	sen-man	せんまん
30	san-jū	さんじゅう		100,000,000	ichi-oku	いちおく
40	yon-jū	よんじゅう				
50	go-jū	ごじゅう		0.76	rei ten nana roku	
60	roku-jū	ろくじゅう			れいてんななろく	
70	nana-jū	ななじゅう				
	shichi-jū	しちじゅう		$\frac{3}{4}$	yon-bun no san	
80	hachi-jū	はちじゅう			よんぶんの　さん	
90	kyū-jū	きゅうじゅう				

131

2. Expressions of time

days of the week

nichi-yōbi にちようび Sunday	getsu-yōbi げつようび Monday	ka-yōbi かようび Tuesday	sui-yōbi すいようび Wednesday

time expression

day	ototoi おととい the day before yesterday	kinō きのう yesterday	kyō きょう today
morning	ototoi no asa おとといの　あさ the morning before last	kinō no asa きのうの　あさ yesterday morning	kesa けさ this morning
night （evening）	ototoi no ban おとといの　ばん the night before last	kinō no ban きのうの　ばん yūbe ゆうべ last night	konban こんばん tonight
week	sensenshū せんせんしゅう (ni-shūkan mae) (にしゅうかん　まえ) the week before last	senshū せんしゅう last week	konshū こんしゅう this week
month	sensengetsu せんせんげつ (ni-kagetsu mae) (にかげつ　まえ) the month before last	sengetsu せんげつ last month	kongetsu こんげつ this month
year	ototoshi おととし the year before last	kyonen きょねん last year	kotoshi ことし this year

moku-yōbi もくようび Thursday	kin-yōbi きんようび Friday	do-yōbi どようび Saturday	nan-yōbi なんようび what day of the week

ashita あした tomorrow	asatte あさって the day after tomorrow	mainichi まいにち everyday
ashita no asa あしたの　あさ tomorrow morning	asatte no asa あさっての　あさ the morning after next	maiasa まいあさ every morning
ashita no ban あしたの　ばん tomorrow night	asatte no ban あさっての　ばん the night after next	maiban まいばん every night
raishū らいしゅう next week	saraishū さらいしゅう the week after next	maishū まいしゅう every week
raigetsu らいげつ next month	saraigetsu さらいげつ the month after next	maitsuki まいつき every month
rainen らいねん next year	sarainen さらいねん the year after next	mainen まいねん maitoshi まいとし every year

telling time

	o'clock		minute
1	ichi-ji いちじ one o'clock	1	ip-pun いっぷん one minute
2	ni-ji にじ	2	ni-fun にふん
3	san-ji さんじ	3	san-pun さんぷん
4	yo-ji よじ	4	yon-pun よんぷん
5	go-ji ごじ	5	go-fun ごふん
6	roku-ji ろくじ	6	rop-pun ろっぷん
7	shichi-ji しちじ	7	nana-fun, shichi-fun ななふん, しちふん
8	hachi-ji はちじ	8	hap-pun はっぷん
9	ku-ji くじ	9	kyū-fun きゅうふん
10	jū-ji じゅうじ	10	jup-pun, jip-pun じゅっぷん, じっぷん
11	jū ichi-ji じゅういちじ	15	jū go-fun じゅうごふん
12	jū ni-ji じゅうにじ	30	san-jup-pun さんじゅっぷん san-jip-pun さんじっぷん han はん
?	nan-ji なんじ		
		?	nan-pun なんぷん

date

	month
1	ichi-gatsu いちがつ January
2	ni-gatsu にがつ February
3	san-gatsu さんがつ March
4	shi-gatsu しがつ April
5	go-gatsu ごがつ May
6	roku-gatsu ろくがつ June
7	shichi-gatsu しちがつ July
8	hachi-gatsu はちがつ August
9	ku-gatsu くがつ September
10	jū-gatsu じゅうがつ October
11	jū ichi-gatsu じゅういちがつ November
12	jū ni-gatsu じゅうにがつ December
?	nan-gatsu なんがつ Which month

	day		
1	tsuitachi ついたち the first day of a month	17	jū shichi-nichi じゅうしちにち
2	futsuka ふつか	18	jū hachi-nichi じゅうはちにち
3	mikka みっか	19	jū ku-nichi じゅうくにち
4	yokka よっか	20	hatsuka はつか
5	itsuka いつか	21	ni-jū ichi-nichi にじゅういちにち
6	muika むいか	22	ni-jū ni-nichi にじゅうににち
7	nanoka なのか	23	ni-jū san-nichi にじゅうさんにち
8	yōka ようか	24	ni-jū yokka にじゅうよっか
9	kokonoka ここのか	25	ni-jū go-nichi にじゅうごにち
10	tōka とおか	26	ni-jū roku-nichi にじゅうろくにち
11	jū ichi-nichi じゅういちにち	27	ni-jū shichi-nichi にじゅうしちにち
12	jū ni-nichi じゅうににち	28	ni-jū hachi-nichi にじゅうはちにち
13	jū san-nichi じゅうさんにち	29	ni-jū ku-nichi にじゅうくにち
14	jū yokka じゅうよっか	30	san-jū-nichi さんじゅうにち
15	jū go-nichi じゅうごにち	31	san-jū ichi-nichi さんじゅういちにち
16	jū roku-nichi じゅうろくにち	?	nan-nichi なんにち

3. Expressions of period

time duration

	hour	minute
1	ichi-jikan いちじかん one hour	ip-pun いっぷん one minute
2	ni-jikan にじかん	ni-fun にふん
3	san-jikan さんじかん	san-pun さんぷん
4	yo-jikan よじかん	yon-pun よんぷん
5	go-jikan ごじかん	go-fun ごふん
6	roku-jikan ろくじかん	rop-pun ろっぷん
7	nana-jikan ななじかん shichi-jikan しちじかん	nana-fun なあふん shichi-fun しちふん
8	hachi-jikan はちじかん	hap-pun はっぷん
9	ku-jikan くじかん	kyū-fun きゅうふん
10	jū-jikan じゅうじかん	jup-pun じゅっぷん jip-pun じっぷん
?	nan-jikan なんじかん	nan-pun なんぷん

period

	day
1	ichi-nichi いちにち one day
2	futsuka ふつか
3	mikka みっか
4	yokka よっか
5	itsuka いつか
6	muika むいか
7	nanoka なのか
8	yōka ようか
9	kokonoka ここのか
10	tōka とおか
?	nan-nichi なんにち

136

week	month	year
is-shūkan いっしゅうかん one week	**ik-kagetsu** いっかげつ one month	**ichi-nen** いちねん one year
ni-shūkan にしゅうかん	**ni-kagetsu** にかげつ	**ni-nen** にねん
san-shūkan さんしゅうかん	**san-kagetsu** さんかげつ	**san-nen** さんねん
yon-shūkan よんしゅうかん	**yon-kagetsu** よんかげつ	**yo-nen** よねん
go-shūkan ごしゅうかん	**go-kagetsu** ごかげつ	**go-nen** ごねん
roku-shūkan ろくしゅうかん	**rok-kagetsu** ろっかげつ **hantoshi** はんとし	**roku-nen** ろくねん
nana-shūkan ななしゅうかん **shichi-shūkan** しちしゅうかん	**nana-kagetsu** ななかげつ **shichi-kagetsu** しちかげつ	**nana-nen** ななねん **shichi-nen** しちねん
has-shūkan はっしゅうかん	**hachi-kagetsu** はちかげつ **hak-kagetsu** はっかげつ	**hachi-nen** はちねん
kyū-shūkan きゅうしゅうかん	**kyu-kagetsu** きゅうかげつ	**kyū-nen** きゅうねん **ku-nen** くねん
jus-shūkan じゅっしゅうかん **jis-shūkan** じっしゅうかん	**juk-kagetsu** じゅっかげつ **jik-kagetsu** じっかげつ	**jū-nen** じゅうねん
nan-shūkan なんしゅうかん	**nan-kagetsu** なんかげつ	**nan-nen** なんねん

4. Counters

	thing		person		thin thing e.g. paper, plate	
1	hitotsu	ひとつ	hitori	ひとり	ichi-mai	いちまい
2	futatsu	ふたつ	futari	ふたり	ni-mai	にまい
3	mittsu	みっつ	san-nin	さんにん	san-mai	さんまい
4	yottsu	よっつ	yo-nin	よにん	yon-mai	よんまい
5	itsutsu	いつつ	go-nin	ごにん	go-mai	ごまい
6	muttsu	むっつ	roku-nin	ろくにん	roku-mai	ろくまい
7	nanatsu	ななつ	nana-nin shichi-nin	ななにん しちにん	nana-mai	ななまい
8	yattsu	やっつ	hachi-nin	はちにん	hachi-mai	はちまい
9	kokonotsu	ここのつ	kyū-nin	きゅうにん	kyū-mai	きゅうまい
10	tō	とお	jū-nin	じゅうにん	jū-mai	じゅうまい
?	ikutsu	いくつ	nan-nin	なんにん	nan-mai	なんまい

	vehicle, machinery		frequency		floor of a building	
1	ichi-dai	いちだい	ik-kai	いっかい	ik-kai	いっかい
2	ni-dai	にだい	ni-kai	にかい	ni-kai	にかい
3	san-dai	さんだい	san-kai	さんかい	san-gai	さんがい
4	yon-dai	よんだい	yon-kai	よんかい	yon-kai	よんかい
5	go-dai	ごだい	go-kai	ごかい	go-kai	ごかい
6	roku-dai	ろくだい	rok-kai	ろっかい	rok-kai	ろっかい
7	nana-dai	ななだい	nana-kai	ななかい	nana-kai	ななかい
8	hachi-dai	はちだい	hak-kai	はっかい	hak-kai	はっかい
9	kyū-dai	きゅうだい	kyū-kai	きゅうかい	kyū-kai	きゅうかい
10	jū-dai	じゅうだい	juk-kai	じゅっかい	juk-kai	じゅっかい
?	nan-dai	なんだい	nan-kai	なんかい	nan-gai	なんがい

order		age		book	
ichi-ban	いちばん	is-sai	いっさい	is-satsu	いっさつ
ni-ban	にばん	ni-sai	にさい	ni-satsu	にさつ
san-ban	さんばん	san-sai	さんさい	san-satsu	さんさつ
yon-ban	よんばん	yon-sai	よんさい	yon-satsu	よんさつ
go-ban	ごばん	go-sai	ごさい	go-satsu	ごさつ
roku-ban	ろくばん	roku-sai	ろくさい	roku-satsu	ろくさつ
nana-ban	ななばん	nana-sai	ななさい	nana-satsu	ななさつ
hachi-ban	はちばん	has-sai	はっさい	has-satsu	はっさつ
kyū-ban	きゅうばん	kyū-sai	きゅうさい	kyū-satsu	きゅうさつ
jū-ban	じゅうばん	jus-sai	じゅっさい	jus-satsu	じゅっさつ
nan-ban	なんばん	nan-sai	なんさい	nan-satsu	なんさつ

139

small thing e.g. egg, orange		drinks and so on which are in cups etc.		long thing e.g. pencil, bottle	
ik-ko	いっこ	ip-pai	いっぱい	ip-pon	いっぽん
ni-ko	にこ	ni-hai	にはい	ni-hon	にほん
san-ko	さんこ	san-bai	さんばい	san-bon	さんぼん
yon-ko	よんこ	yon-hai	よんはい	yon-hon	よんほん
go-ko	ごこ	go-hai	ごはい	go-hon	ごほん
rok-ko	ろっこ	rop-pai	ろっぱい	rop-pon	ろっぽん
nana-ko	ななこ	nana-hai	ななはい	nana-hon	ななほん
hak-ko	はっこ	hap-pai	はっぱい	hap-pon	はっぽん
kyū-ko	きゅうこ	kyū-hai	きゅうはい	kyū-hon	きゅうほん
juk-ko	じゅっこ	jup-pai	じゅっぱい	jup-pon	じゅっぽん
nan-ko	なんこ	nan-bai	なんばい	nan-bon	なんぼん

5. Conjugation of verbs

I -gurūpu

	masu-kei		te-kei	jisho-kei
aimasu [tomodachi ni ～] あいます	ai	masu	atte	a
araimasu　あらいます	arai	masu	aratte	ara
arimasu　あります	ari	masu	atte	ar
arimasu　あります	ari	masu	atte	ar
arukimasu　あるきます	aruki	masu	aruite	aruk
asobimasu　あそびます	asobi	masu	asonde	asob
dashimasu　だします	dashi	masu	dashite	das
furimasu [ame ga ～] ふります	furi	masu	futte	fur
ganbarimasu　がんばります	ganbari	masu	ganbatte	ganbar
hairimasu [heya ni ～] はいります	hairi	masu	haitte	hair
hakimasu　はきます	haki	masu	haite	hak
hanashimasu　はなします	hanashi	masu	hanashite	hanas
haraimasu　はらいます	harai	masu	haratte	hara
hatarakimasu　はたらきます	hataraki	masu	hataraite	hatarak
hikimasu [piano o ～] ひきます	hiki	masu	hiite	hik
iimasu　いいます	ii	masu	itte	i
ikimasu　いきます	iki	masu	itte	ik
irimasu [jisho ga ～] いります	iri	masu	itte	ir
isogimasu　いそぎます	isogi	masu	isoide	isog
kaburimasu　かぶります	kaburi	masu	kabutte	kabur
kaerimasu　かえります	kaeri	masu	kaette	kaer
kaeshimasu　かえします	kaeshi	masu	kaeshite	kaes
kaimasu　かいます	kai	masu	katte	ka
kakarimasu　かかります	kakari	masu	kakatte	kakar
kakimasu　かきます	kaki	masu	kaite	kak
kashimasu　かします	kashi	masu	kashite	kas

nai-kei	ta-kei	imi	ka
awa nai	atta	meet [a friend]	6
arawa nai	aratta	wash	1 6
nai	atta	have	9
nai	atta	exist (inanimate things)	1 0
aruka nai	aruita	walk	1 6
asoba nai	asonda	play, enjoy oneself	1 3
dasa nai	dashita	take out, hand in	1 7
fura nai	futta	rain	1 4
ganbara nai	ganbatta	do one's best	2 3
haira nai	haitta	enter [a room]	1 3
haka nai	haita	wear (shoes, etc.)	2 2
hanasa nai	hanashita	speak	1 4
harawa nai	haratta	pay	1 7
hataraka nai	hataraita	work	4
hika nai	hiita	play [the piano]	1 8
iwa nai	itta	say	1 4
ika nai	itta	go	5
ira nai	itta	need [a dictionary]	2 0
isoga nai	isoida	hurry	1 4
kabura nai	kabutta	put on (hat etc.)	2 2
kaera nai	kaetta	go home, return	5
kaesa nai	kaeshita	give back, return (things)	1 7
kawa nai	katta	buy	6
kakara nai	kakatta	take (time)	1 1
kaka nai	kaita	write, draw, paint	6
kasa nai	kashita	lend	7

		masu-kei		te-kei	jisho-kei
keshimasu	けします	keshi	masu	keshite	ke
kikimasu	ききます	kiki	masu	kiite	ki
kikimasu [sensei ni ~]	ききます	kiki	masu	kiite	ki
kirimasu	きります	kiri	masu	kitte	ki
kirimasu [suitchi o ~]	きります	kiri	masu	kitte	ki
komarimasu	こまります	komari	masu	komatte	koma
machimasu	まちます	machi	masu	matte	mat
magarimasu [migi e ~]	まがります	magari	masu	magatte	maga
mawashimasu	まわします	mawashi	masu	mawashite	mawa
mochimasu	もちます	mochi	masu	motte	mot
moraimasu	もらいます	morai	masu	moratte	mora
motte ikimasu	もって いきます	motte iki	masu	motte itte	motte i
nakushimasu	なくします	nakushi	masu	nakushite	naku
naoshimasu	なおします	naoshi	masu	naoshite	nao
naoshimasu	なおします	naoshi	masu	naoshite	nao
naraimasu	ならいます	narai	masu	naratte	nara
narimasu	なります	nari	masu	natte	na
nomimasu	のみます	nomi	masu	nonde	nom
norimasu [densha ni ~]	のります	nori	masu	notte	no
nugimasu	ぬぎます	nugi	masu	nuide	nug
okimasu	おきます	oki	masu	oite	ok
okurimasu [nimotsu o ~]	おくります	okuri	masu	okutte	oku
okurimasu [hito o ~]	おくります	okuri	masu	okutte	oku
omoimasu	おもいます	omoi	masu	omotte	omo
oshimasu	おします	oshi	masu	oshite	os
owarimasu	おわります	owari	masu	owatte	owa

nai-kei	ta-kei	imi	ka
kesa nai	keshita	switch off	1 5
kika nai	kiita	listen, hear	6
kika nai	kiita	ask [the teacher]	2 3
kira nai	kitta	cut	7
kira nai	kitta	switch off	2 5
komara nai	komatta	have a problem	2 3
mata nai	matta	wait	1 4
magara nai	magatta	turn [right]	2 3
mawasa nai	mawashita	rotate (vt.), turn (vt.)	2 3
mota nai	motta	hold	1 5
morawa nai	moratta	receive	7
motte ika nai	motte itta	take (something)	2 2
nakusa nai	nakushita	lose	1 7
naosa nai	naoshita	repair	1 8
naosa nai	naoshita	correct (a mistake)	2 5
narawa nai	naratta	learn	7
nara nai	natta	become	1 9
noma nai	nonda	drink	6
nora nai	notta	get [a train]	1 6
nuga nai	nuida	take off (clothes, shoes, etc.)	1 7
oka nai	oita	put	1 5
okura nai	okutta	send [baggage, parcel]	1 3
okura nai	okutta	see [someone] home	2 4
omowa nai	omotta	think	2 1
osa nai	oshita	push, press	2 3
owara nai	owatta	finish	4

143

		masu-kei		te-kei	jisho-kei
oyogimasu	およぎます	oyogi	masu	oyoide	oyog
sawarimasu [kikai ni ~] さわります		sawari	masu	sawatte	sawa
shirimasu	しります	shiri	masu	shitte	shi
suimasu [tabako o ~] すいます		sui	masu	sutte	su
sumimasu	すみます	sumi	masu	sunde	sum
suwarimasu [isu ni ~] すわります		suwari	masu	suwatte	suwa
tachimasu	たちます	tachi	masu	tatte	tats
tetsudaimasu	てつだいます	tetsudai	masu	tetsudatte	tetsuda
tomarimasu [hoteru ni ~] とまります		tomari	masu	tomatte	toma
tomarimasu [kikai ga ~] とまります		tomari	masu	tomatte	toma
torimasu [shashin o ~] とります		tori	masu	totte	to
torimasu	とります	tori	masu	totte	to
tsukaimasu	つかいます	tsukai	masu	tsukatte	tsuka
tsukurimasu	つくります	tsukuri	masu	tsukutte	tsuku
tsurete ikimasu	つれて いきます	tsurete iki	masu	tsurete itte	tsurete ik
ugokimasu [kikai ga ~] うごきます		ugoki	masu	ugoite	ugok
urimasu	うります	uri	masu	utte	u
utaimasu	うたいます	utai	masu	utatte	uta
wakarimasu	わかります	wakari	masu	wakatte	waka
watarimasu [michi o ~] わたります		watari	masu	watatte	wata
yaku ni tachimasu やくに たちます		yaku ni tachi	masu	yaku ni tatte	yaku ni tats
yasumimasu	やすみます	yasumi	masu	yasunde	yasum
yobimasu	よびます	yobi	masu	yonde	yob
yomimasu	よみます	yomi	masu	yonde	yom

144

nai-kei	ta-kei	imi	ka
oyoga nai	oyoida	swim	1 8
sawara nai	sawatta	touch [a machine]	1 7
shira nai	shitta	get to know	1 5
suwa nai	sutta	smoke	6
suma nai	sunda	be going to live	1 5
suwara nai	suwatta	sit down [on a chair]	1 5
tata nai	tatta	stand up	1 5
tetsudawa nai	tetsudatta	help (with a task)	1 4
tomara nai	tomatta	stay [at a hotel]	1 9
tomara nai	tomatta	[a machine] stop	2 3
tora nai	totta	take [a photo]	6
tora nai	totta	take	1 4
tsukawa nai	tsukatta	use	1 5
tsukura nai	tsukutta	make, produce	1 5
tsurete ika nai	tsurete itta	take (someone) everywhere	2 4
ugoka nai	ugoita	[a machine] move, work	2 3
ura nai	utta	sell	1 5
utawa nai	utatta	sing	1 8
wakara nai	wakatta	understand	9
watara nai	watatta	cross [a road]	2 3
yaku ni tata nai	yaku ni tatta	be useful	2 1
yasuma nai	yasunda	take a rest, rest	4
yoba nai	yonda	call	1 4
yoma nai	yonda	read	6

II -gurūpu

		masu-kei		te-kei	jisho-kei
abimasu [shawā o ～] あびます		abi	masu	abite	abir
agemasu	あげます	age	masu	agete	ager
akemasu	あけます	ake	masu	akete	aker
dekakemasu	でかけます	dekake	masu	dekakete	dekaker
dekimasu	できます	deki	masu	dekite	dekir
demasu [heya o ～] でます		de	masu	dete	der
demasu [kippu ga ～] でます		de	masu	dete	der
hajimemasu	はじめます	hajime	masu	hajimete	hajimer
imasu	います	i	masu	ite	ir
imasu [kodomo ga ～] います		i	masu	ite	ir
imasu [Nihon ni ～] います		i	masu	ite	ir
iremasu	いれます	ire	masu	irete	irer
iremasu [suitchi o ～] いれます		ire	masu	irete	irer
kaemasu	かえます	kae	masu	kaete	kaer
kakemasu [denwa o ～] かけます		kake	masu	kakete	kaker
kakemasu [megane o ～] かけます		kake	masu	kakete	kaker
kangaemasu	かんがえます	kangae	masu	kangaete	kangaer
karimasu	かります	kari	masu	karite	karir
katazukemasu	かたづけます	katazuke	masu	katazukete	katazuker
kimasu [shatsu o ～] きます		ki	masu	kite	kir
ki o tsukemasu [kuruma ni ～] きを つけます		ki o tsuke	masu	ki o tsukete	ki o tsuker
kuremasu	くれます	kure	masu	kurete	kurer
mimasu	みます	mi	masu	mite	mir
misemasu	みせます	mise	masu	misete	miser
motte imasu	もって います	motte i	masu	motte ite	motte ir

nai-kei		ta-kei	imi	ka
abi	nai	abita	take [a shower]	1 6
age	nai	ageta	give	7
ake	nai	aketa	open	1 5
dekake	nai	dekaketa	go out (of a house)	1 9
deki	nai	dekita	be able to	1 8
de	nai	deta	go out [of the room]	1 3
de	nai	deta	[a ticket] come out	2 3
hajime	nai	hajimeta	begin (vt.)	1 8
i	nai	ita	exist (living things)	1 0
i	nai	ita	have [a child]	1 1
i	nai	ita	stay, be [in Japan]	1 1
ire	nai	ireta	put in	1 7
ire	nai	ireta	switch on	2 5
kae	nai	kaeta	change	1 3
kake	nai	kaketa	make a phone call	7
kake	nai	kaketa	wear [glasses]	2 2
kangae	nai	kangaeta	think	2 5
kari	nai	karita	borrow	7
katazuke	nai	katazuketa	put (things) in order, tidy up	2 5
ki	nai	kita	wear (a shirt, etc.)	2 2
ki o tsuke	nai	ki o tsuketa	pay attention [to a car]	1 7
kure	nai	kureta	give something (to me)	2 4
mi	nai	mita	see	6
mise	nai	miseta	show	1 4
motte i	nai	motte ita	have, possess	1 5

		masu-kei		te-kei	jisho-kei
nemasu	ねます	ne	masu	nete	ne
norikaemasu	のりかえます	norikae	masu	norikaete	norikae
oboemasu	おぼえます	oboe	masu	oboete	oboe
okimasu	おきます	oki	masu	okite	oki
orimasu [densha o ～] おります		ori	masu	orite	ori
oshiemasu	おしえます	oshie	masu	oshiete	oshie
oshiemasu	おしえます	oshie	masu	oshiete	oshie
shimemasu	しめます	shime	masu	shimete	shime
shirabemasu	しらべます	shirabe	masu	shirabete	shirabe
shitte imasu	しって います	shitte i	masu	shitte ite	shitte
sunde imasu [Tōkyō ni ～] すんで います		sunde i	masu	sunde ite	sunde
tabemasu	たべます	tabe	masu	tabete	tabe
tomemasu	とめます	tome	masu	tomete	tome
tsukemasu	つけます	tsuke	masu	tsukete	tsuke
tsuzukemasu	つづけます	tsuzuke	masu	tsuzukete	tsuzuke
wasuremasu	わすれます	wasure	masu	wasurete	wasure
yamemasu	やめます	yame	masu	yamete	yame

nai-kei	ta-kei	imi	ka
ne nai	neta	sleep, go to bed	4
norikae nai	norikaeta	change (trains)	1 6
oboe nai	oboeta	memorize, remember	1 4
oki nai	okita	get up	4
ori nai	orita	get off [a train]	1 6
oshie nai	oshieta	teach	7
oshie nai	oshieta	tell	1 4
shime nai	shimeta	shut	1 5
shirabe nai	shirabeta	check up, investigate	2 5
shitte i nai	shitte ita	know	1 5
sunde i nai	sunde ita	live [in Tokyo]	1 5
tabe nai	tabeta	eat	6
tome nai	tometa	stop, park (a car)	1 7
tsuke nai	tsuketa	switch on	1 5
tsuzuke nai	tsuzuketa	continue	2 5
wasure nai	wasureta	forget	1 7
yame nai	yameta	stop (studying), resign (one's company)	2 5

III -gurūpu

	masu-kei		te-kei	jisho-kei
annai-shimasu あんないします	annai-shi	masu	annai-shite	annai-su
benkyō-shimasu べんきょうします	benkyō-shi	masu	benkyō-shite	benkyō-su
chōsetsu-shimasu ちょうせつします	chōsetsu-shi	masu	chōsetsu-shite	chōsetsu-su
jisshū-shimasu じっしゅうします	jisshū-shi	masu	jisshū-shite	jisshū-su
kaimono-shimasu かいものします	kaimono-shi	masu	kaimono-shite	kaimono-su
kekkon-shimasu けっこんします	kekkon-shi	masu	kekkon-shite	kekkon-su
kenbutsu-shimasu [machi o ～] けんぶつします	kenbutsu-shi	masu	kenbutsu-shite	kenbutsu-su
kengaku-shimasu [kōjō o ～] けんがくします	kengaku-shi	masu	kengaku-shite	kengaku-su
kimasu きます	ki	masu	kite	ku
kopii-shimasu コピーします	kopii-shi	masu	kopii-shite	kopii-su
motte kimasu もって きます	motte ki	masu	motte kite	motte ku
renshū-shimasu れんしゅうします	renshū-shi	masu	renshū-shite	renshū-su
sanpo-shimasu [kōen o ～] さんぽします	sanpo-shi	masu	sanpo-shite	sanpo-su
sentaku-shimasu せんたくします	sentaku-shi	masu	sentaku-shite	sentaku-su
setsumei-shimasu せつめいします	setsumei-shi	masu	setsumei-shite	setsumei-su
shimasu します	shi	masu	shite	su
shimasu [pinpon o ～] します	shi	masu	shite	su
shinpai-shimasu しんぱいします	shinpai-shi	masu	shinpai-shite	shinpai-su
shōkai-shimasu しょうかいします	shōkai-shi	masu	shōkai-shite	shōkai-su
shokuji-shimasu しょくじします	shokuji-shi	masu	shokuji-shite	shokuji-su
shūri-shimasu しゅうりします	shūri-shi	masu	shūri-shite	shūri-su
sōji-shimasu そうじします	sōji-shi	masu	sōji-shite	sōji-su
tsurete kimasu つれて きます	tsurete ki	masu	tsurete kite	tsurete ku
unten-shimasu うんてんします	unten-shi	masu	unten-shite	unten-su

nai-kei		ta-kei	imi	ka
annai-shi	nai	annai-shita	show around, show the way	2 4
benkyō-shi	nai	benkyō-shita	study	4
chōsetsu-shi	nai	chōsetsu-shita	adjust	2 3
jisshū-shi	nai	jisshū-shita	do practical training	6
kaimono-shi	nai	kaimono-shita	do shopping	1 3
kekkon-shi	nai	kekkon-shita	get married	1 3
kenbutsu-shi	nai	kenbutsu-shita	do sightseeing [in a town]	1 3
kengaku-shi	nai	kengaku-shita	visit [a factory]	1 3
ko	nai	kita	come	5
kopii-shi	nai	kopii-shita	make a photo copy	2 4
motte ko	nai	motte kita	bring (something)	2 2
renshū-shi	nai	renshū-shita	practise	1 8
sanpo-shi	nai	sanpo-shita	take a walk [in a park]	1 3
sentaku-shi	nai	sentaku-shita	wash (clothes etc.)	1 9
setsumei-shi	nai	setsumei-shita	explain	2 4
shi	nai	shita	do	6
shi	nai	shita	play [table tennis]	6
shinpai-shi	nai	shinpai-shita	worry	1 7
shōkai-shi	nai	shōkai-shita	introduce	2 4
shokuji-shi	nai	shokuji-shita	have a meal, dine	1 6
shūri-shi	nai	shūri-shita	repair	7
sōji-shi	nai	sōji-shita	clean (a room, etc.)	1 9
tsurete ko	nai	tsurete kita	bring (someone)	2 4
unten-shi	nai	unten-shita	drive	1 8

新 日 本 語 の 基 礎 I
〈分冊 英語訳〉

1990年 1 月31日　初 版 発 行
1991年 4 月10日　第 3 刷発行

編集　財団法人　海外技術者研修協会
発行　株式会社　スリーエーネットワーク
　　　〒101 東京都千代田区猿楽町2-6-3(松栄ビル)
　　　電話・東京03(3292)5751(代表)
印刷　株式会社　東京アド・ソース

ISBN4-906224-52-0 C0081